VSAM for the COBOL Programmer

VSAM for the COBOL Programmer

Concepts·COBOL·JCL·IDCAMS

DOUG LOWE

Mike Murach & Associates, Inc.

4222 West Alamos, Suite 101
Fresno, California 93711
(209) 275-3335

Printed in the United States of America.

20 19 18 17 16 15 14 13 12 11 10 9

ISBN 0-911625-12-7

Contents

Preface

If you are a COBOL programmer involved in the development of a VSAM system, or if you are involved in the conversion of an existing ISAM system, or if you work at a VS installation that is considering converting to VSAM, this book is for you. This book presents everything a COBOL programmer needs to know about VSAM. So with this book in hand, you will rarely need to consult an IBM VSAM manual.

This book covers the nuts and bolts of VSAM. It is designed to get you started writing VSAM programs right away. As a result, I purposely omitted those features of VSAM that are rarely (if ever) used by COBOL programmers—features such as alternate indexing and dynamic access. And I omitted a great deal of the detail that is rarely a concern of the COBOL programmer—details such as how to select the most efficient control interval size or how to code an exception routine in assembler language. Instead, I have kept my sights set on a usable "professional subset" of VSAM. So in this book you will find the information you need to know without having to sift through a great deal of information you don't need to know.

To make it easy for you to learn COBOL for VSAM files, this book includes seven complete program listings. These programs show you how to perform the vast majority of VSAM file handling functions...file loading, sequential and random updating, report preparation, and so on. Once you have mastered the COBOL elements for VSAM files, these programs become models that you can use when you write your own VSAM programs.

How to use this book

This book consists of four parts. Part 1 provides an introduction to VSAM, including a summary of the advantages and disadvantages of VSAM and an introduction to the terminology used in the rest of the book. Part 2 presents the COBOL and JCL elements you need to know for VSAM indexed files. Since 95 percent or more of all VSAM files are indexed files, this part is the meat of the book. Once you have mastered the material in part 2, you are ready to begin programming for VSAM files. Then, part 3 provides an introduction to the other two kinds of VSAM files: sequential and relative. And part 4 explains the specific variations a DOS user should be aware of.

As an appendix, I have included a guide for converting ISAM programs to VSAM. There, you will find a listing of ISAM elements that must be changed or deleted for VSAM, as well as VSAM elements that must be added. This, of course, is an invaluable tool for any VSAM conversion effort.

Because learning depends on what you do more than on what you see or hear, there are self-checking aids and exercises at the end of each topic in this book. Specifically, each topic is followed by terminology lists, behavioral objectives, and whenever relevant, problems and their solutions.

The terminology lists provide listings of the new words presented in the text of each topic. The intent is not that you be able to define words, but that you feel you understand them. So after you read a topic, you can glance at the list and note any word whose meaning is unclear to you. Then, you can reread the related material.

The behavioral objectives describe the activities you should be able to do when you complete the topic. The theory is that you will be a more effective learner if you know what you are expected to do. Most of the objectives in this book ask you to apply the knowledge rather than just list, describe, or explain what you've learned.

For each objective that asks you to apply what you've learned, you will find a problem and its solution. If there is one message that is clear from research in education, it is that real learning is a result of what the learner does—not the result of what he sees, hears, or reads. The problems are intended to get you involved so that you will go beyond a superficial knowledge of VSAM to a deeper understanding of VSAM.

Solutions are presented right after the problems rather than at the end of the book or in a supplement. This has the advantage of letting you know that you are right when you are right, and, more importantly, of letting you know right away when you are wrong. By checking the solution when you finish a problem, you can discover your mistakes and correct false notions right away.

A special note for DOS users

All of the programming examples in chapters 1-5 of this book were tested on a 3033 running under OS/MVS. As a result, chapters 1-5 are oriented towards OS users. Chapter 6 presents the major variations you will encounter if you are using VSAM on a DOS system (DOS/VS or VSE). Chapter 6 is organized in the same manner as the rest of the book. So after reading a particular topic in chapters 1-5, you can turn to the appropriate section of chapter 6 to learn about the variations for DOS (if there are any). In many cases, VSAM is the same whether you are using OS or DOS. And when there are variations, they are usually minor. But you should always check in chapter 6 to be sure.

Related products

This book supplements a two-part series for COBOL training: *Structured ANS COBOL, Part 1* and *Part 2*, by Mike Murach and Paul Noll. The first book, *Structured ANS COBOL, Part 1*, teaches a professional subset of COBOL that includes JCL and COBOL for sequential files (non-VSAM). In brief, a student who completes *Part 1* will have the qualifications of an entry-level programmer in industry. The second book, *Structured ANS COBOL, Part 2*, is designed to train an entry-level programmer to use advanced COBOL features such as table handling, subprograms, the COPY library, the debugging verbs, sort, and indexed file handling (ISAM). Since many practicing programmers don't have some of these skills, this course may be of value to them as well as to entry-level programmers.

This VSAM book requires chapters 1-5 in *Part 1* and chapter 9 in *Part 2* as background. In other words, this book assumes that you have a working knowledge of COBOL including ISAM file handling before you begin. Of course, it isn't necessary that you obtain that background from our books; you may well have been prepared by some other course or experience.

The examples in this book are presented within the context of structured programming as presented in Paul Noll's book, *Structured Programming for the COBOL Programmer*. This book presents a practical method for designing, documenting, coding, and testing structured programs in COBOL. *Structured ANS COBOL, Part 1* and *Part 2*, both give a brief presentation of this method. If you are familiar with structured programming techniques, you will find that the use of VSAM files presents no added structural complexity. On the other hand, if you don't use structured programming techniques, you can still learn VSAM file handling from this book because all of its examples are highly readable.

If you are interested in any of our other books, you can write, call, or use the order form near the back of this book. If you don't find them—or this book, for that matter—worth many times more than your purchase price, you can return them at any time for a full refund.

Conclusion

I hope you find this book both readable and useful. As soon as you finish chapters 1-3, you should be able to write COBOL programs for VSAM files without using any other reference materials. And you should be able to convert existing ISAM programs to VSAM, using the appendix as a guide.

As always, we welcome your comments, criticisms, suggestions, or questions. If you have any, feel free to use the postage-paid comment form near the back of the book. Your opinions really do count.

Doug Lowe
Fresno, California
September, 1981

PART ONE

Required Background

This part presents what you need to know before you can begin to write COBOL programs for VSAM files. The chapter in this part presents the advantages and disadvantages of using VSAM and an introduction to the terminology used throughout the book. If you are already convinced of the advantages of VSAM, and are already familiar with VSAM terminology, you can go directly to part 2. Otherwise, I suggest you read chapter 1.

IBM

1

An Introduction to VSAM

This chapter presents what you need to know before you can start learning how to write COBOL programs for VSAM. At the outset, you should *want* to use VSAM files. So topic 1 of this chapter discusses the advantages and disadvantages of VSAM. Even if you're already convinced you should be using VSAM, I urge you to read this topic. Many installations have converted to VSAM without really understanding its benefits—and its drawbacks.

Topic 2 introduces many of the terms used in the rest of the book. If you're already familiar with this terminology through a previous course or job experience, you should check the terminology list and objectives at the end of topic 2. If you feel comfortable with them, you can move along to part 2. If not, please read topic 2.

TOPIC 1 Why VSAM?

For ten years, IBM's Indexed Sequential Access Method (ISAM) was the most popular indexed file handling technique in the industry. And for ten years ISAM users complained about its inefficiency. So in the mid-1970s, IBM announced a new indexed file handling technique: the Virtual Storage Access Method (VSAM). Unfortunately, VSAM did not meet all of its expectations. As a result, not all VS users have converted to VSAM. This topic discusses the advantages and disadvantages of using VSAM. It points out why System/370 users should convert their files to VSAM, as well as why many of them haven't.

The advantages of VSAM

The greatest advantage of using VSAM is that it is much more efficient than ISAM. Two things make VSAM indexed files more efficient than ISAM. First, the entire index structure of a VSAM file is generally processed in virtual storage; on an ISAM file, only the highest level of the index is processed in main storage—and even that only happens if the program specifies the APPLY CORE-INDEX option for the file. Naturally, the index can be processed much more rapidly in virtual storage than it can on the disk. Second, VSAM eliminates the bothersome overflow areas used for ISAM files. In an ISAM file, additions are stored in separate disk locations. Periodically, the ISAM file must be reorganized so the records in the overflow areas are moved into their proper locations in the file. If the file isn't reorganized often enough (and most ISAM files aren't), it becomes very time-consuming to process the file. In contrast, VSAM reduces this problem by embedding free space in the file so that additions are placed where they belong. As a result, overflow areas aren't required by VSAM.

Just how much more efficient is VSAM than ISAM? Consider one test in which an ISAM file and a VSAM file, each containing 6,000 500-byte records (no dummy records), were compared. First, the files were read sequentially. During this portion of the test, the ISAM file outperformed the VSAM file by about 4 percent (elapsed execution time). Then, the files were updated with 1,200 random additions. For this portion of the test, the elapsed execution time for the VSAM file was less than half—47 percent—of the execution time for the ISAM file. In other words, the VSAM update program ran more than twice as fast as the ISAM update program. After the files had been updated, they were read again sequentially. This time, the VSAM file outperformed the ISAM file by 22 percent (again, elapsed execution time). After the random additions, the ISAM file lost its slight edge over the VSAM file.

A second advantage of VSAM is the way it uses its catalogs. Under VSAM, *all* files must be cataloged in the VSAM master catalog either directly or indirectly. By directly, I mean that the file is actually referenced by the master catalog. By indirectly, I mean that the master catalog refers to another catalog which in turn refers to the file. Since all VSAM files must be cataloged, many of the problems associated with the standard OS catalog structure are eliminated.

A third advantage of VSAM is its flexibility. A VSAM file may have one of three types of organization: sequential, indexed, or relative. And there is a VSAM utility program that makes it easy to convert a file from one organization to another—a useful feature that isn't readily available for non-VSAM files.

Because of the availability of these three types of file organization, VSAM is said to be usable in either online or batch systems. In a sense, however, neither of these claims means anything to the COBOL programmer. To begin with, COBOL programmers rarely access data files directly in an online system. Instead, they use a package such as CICS to access the files. Although it is true that you can tell CICS whether an indexed file is ISAM or VSAM, this choice has absolutely no effect on how the COBOL programmer writes his programs.

As for batch processing, VSAM isn't really effective as a replacement for all of the files in a batch system. For indexed files, VSAM is much better than ISAM. But it would be a serious mistake to convert non-VSAM sequential files to VSAM. For one thing, VSAM sequential files are no more efficient than non-VSAM sequential files so the conversion would gain nothing in efficiency. Worse yet, many of the features of non-VSAM sequential files that are vital to most batch processing systems are not available with VSAM sequential files. For example, generation processing is not supported by VSAM. And there is no such thing as a temporary file in VSAM—work files have to be cataloged at the beginning of the job and scratched at the end. In short, although ISAM files should be converted to VSAM, sequential files are best kept as non-VSAM files.

A fourth advantage of VSAM is its simplified JCL requirements. All of the functions normally done with JCL at file creation time are handled by a general-purpose utility program for file definition. Once a file is defined, only two JCL parameters are needed to process the file: DSNAME and DISP. Since DISP is always OLD, the only JCL parameter that varies from one VSAM file to the next—regardless of the file's organization—is the data set name. And the file's DD statement is coded the same whether the file is being loaded, read, or updated. (For non-VSAM files, the JCL required to load a file is different than that used to process it later.)

The disadvantages of VSAM

Of course, VSAM is not the perfect access method. I have already mentioned one disadvantage: VSAM sequential files aren't at all useful in most batch processing systems.

Another disadvantage of VSAM is that it is often guilty of wasting disk space because of its large block sizes. For example, each track on a 3350 disk pack is capable of storing over 19,000 bytes.

However, a typical block size for a VSAM file is 4,000 bytes (blocks larger than this must be in multiples of 4K; smaller than this, the processing efficiency of the file drops rapidly). Simple arithmetic tells you that each 19K track will hold four 4K blocks, with 3,000 bytes of wasted space in each track.

One major drawback of VSAM isn't really the fault of VSAM itself but of the VS COBOL compiler (which is the only COBOL compiler that can generate code for VSAM files). Under the older compilers, when a recoverable I/O error—such as a duplicate key or record not found—was encountered, control was returned to the COBOL program via the INVALID KEY clause. Any other I/O errors caused the program to terminate abnormally. In other words, the operating system stepped in on serious errors so the COBOL programmer didn't have to check for those conditions. Under the VS COBOL compiler, however, the operating system doesn't do this for you. Instead, control always returns to the COBOL program—even if a serious I/O error occurs. The nature of the error is indicated by a code passed to a specified field in the COBOL program. You, as a COBOL programmer, are then responsible to use this code to check for I/O errors. If you don't, serious errors could go undetected.

To illustrate, suppose you are performing a file-maintenance job in which 500 records are added to a master file of 5000 records. If some unusual error condition (such as running out of disk space) occurs, and the COBOL program doesn't check for it, all of the additions after the error took place could be lost. Problems of this nature are often difficult to track down and may go undetected for days.

Actually, the situation really isn't as bad as it sounds. In fact, it only takes a few extra lines of code in the COBOL program to check for these errors. The important thing is that COBOL programmers be aware that they must check for error conditions in their COBOL programs.

Conclusion

Although VSAM is not an ideal access method, I recommend that all users of VS systems convert their ISAM files to VSAM as soon as they can. The benefits far outweigh the disadvantages.

Naturally, a conversion of this nature is not to be taken lightly. It is a major decision that must be well thought out. In general, a conversion from ISAM to VSAM involves two phases. In the first phase, the ISAM files are converted to VSAM organization. This is done using a special utility program, described in chapter 3.

The second phase of conversion involves the programs that process the files. This conversion phase usually consists of two steps. First, an interface program is used to allow programs that are coded for ISAM files to process VSAM files. This allows production work to continue while program modifications are being made. The ISAM interface is covered in topic 1 of the next chapter. Second, the ISAM programs are modified so they process VSAM files properly. In topic 2 of the next chapter, you'll see how to make these modifications (and how to develop new programs for VSAM files).

Objectives

1. Describe the advantages and disadvantages of using VSAM instead of ISAM.

TOPIC 2 VSAM Terminology

To begin with, *VSAM* stands for *Virtual Storage Access Method.* And that's just what it is: an access method designed for virtual storage systems. VSAM operates on all of IBM's VS systems—both OS and DOS systems. Although virtual storage is crucial to VSAM's operation, its dependency on virtual storage is strictly transparent to you. So it isn't important that you have an in-depth understanding of how virtual storage works in order to understand how VSAM works.

VSAM provides three types of file organization. An *entry-sequenced data set* (*ESDS*) is like a standard sequential data set (*data set* is an OS term meaning "file"). Its records are processed one at a time in the order in which they were loaded. A *key-sequenced data set* (*KSDS*) is like an ISAM file—its records may be processed sequentially or randomly based on a key value. A key-sequenced file is often called an *indexed file*; in this book, the terms are used interchangeably. A *relative-record data set* (*RRDS*) is like a non-VSAM relative file. Its records can be accessed based on their relative positions in the file. Since entry-sequenced and relative-record files are rarely used, VSAM is usually thought of as a replacement for ISAM.

VSAM areas

VSAM defines the various areas required to maintain its data sets (files) in a much more organized manner than the other access methods. Along with this increased organization comes a whole new set of terminology which you must learn. To begin with, a VSAM data set is called a *cluster*. A cluster consists of a *data component*, which contains the actual records of the file, plus any control areas or indexes associated with the data component. A cluster must be defined by the VSAM utility program, IDCAMS, before the data set may be used. (I'll get to IDCAMS in just a moment.)

Clusters are stored in designated portions of direct-access volumes called *data spaces.* A data space is simply an area of a direct-access volume that is reserved for VSAM files. Every VSAM file is contained in a data space. Non-VSAM files may not be stored in a VSAM data space—they must be outside the data space. A data space must be defined by IDCAMS before a cluster may be stored in it.

One data space may be used to store all of one cluster, part of one cluster, or several clusters. On a single disk volume, there may be one or several data spaces that occupy all or part of the volume. Any area of a disk volume not occupied by a data space may be used to store non-VSAM files. Of course, if the entire volume is filled with data space, no non-VSAM files may be stored on that volume.

Figure 1-1 illustrates a disk volume containing two VSAM data spaces. The first data space contains two clusters (an accounts receivable master file and a payroll master file) and two areas of free space. The second data space contains a customer master file and free space. The free areas in the data space are reserved for additional VSAM files or expansion of the existing VSAM files. The areas of the volume not included in the data spaces may be used for non-VSAM data sets.

The unit of direct-access storage that VSAM transfers between disk storage and virtual storage when an I-O request is made is called a *control interval.* A control interval may contain one or several records. In addition, a single record may occupy more than one control interval (this is called a *spanned record*). Within a control interval, the records may be fixed or variable in length. However, the control interval itself is always of a fixed length assigned by VSAM on the basis of record size and disk characteristics. Although you can override VSAM's selection of control interval size, it is usually best not to.

In many ways, the control interval is similar to the concept of blocking for non-VSAM files. However, a control interval contains control information that isn't found in a block. In addition, part of a control interval may be left empty, so that additions to the file may be made easily. This normally isn't done with non-VSAM blocked files.

A group of contiguous (that is, adjacent) control intervals forms a *control area* within a data space. When a VSAM cluster is defined, a control area is usually preformatted so that the file may be processed more efficiently. In the same way that portions of a control interval may be left empty, entire control intervals within a control area may be set aside for file additions.

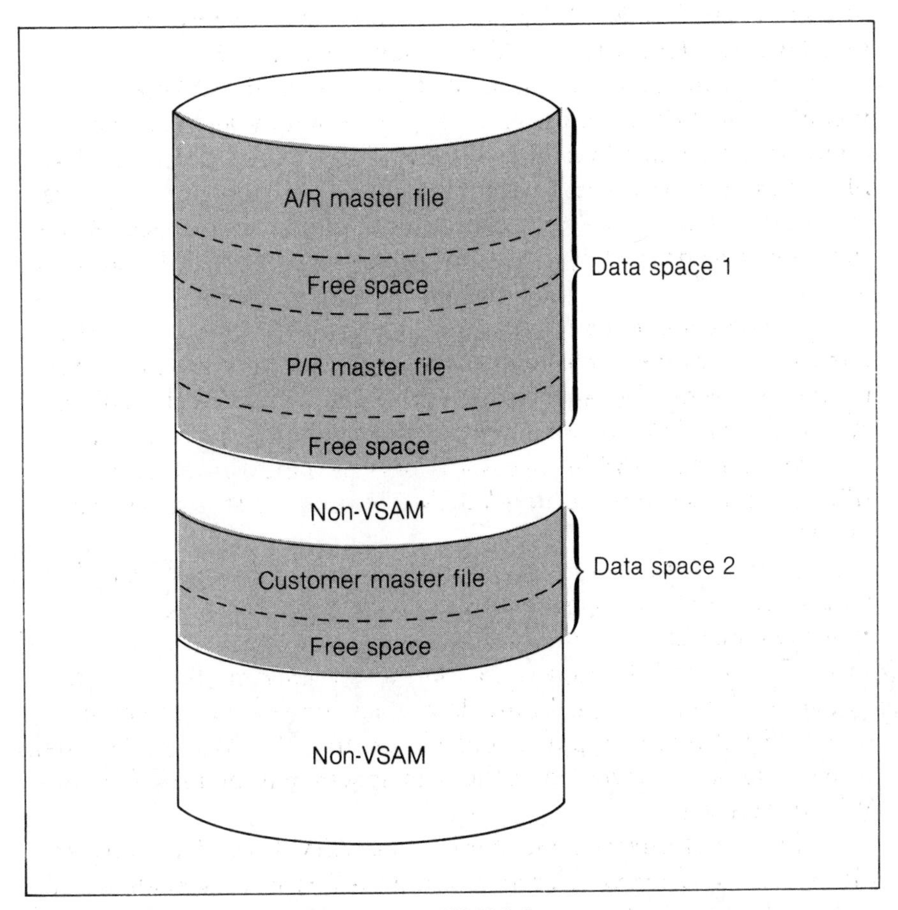

Figure 1-1 Disk volume containing two VSAM data spaces

Figure 1-2 illustrates the structure of a VSAM data component. Several control areas make up the data component of a cluster. Within each control area are several control intervals, each containing data records and control information. Of course, in an actual production file, the data component will consist of many control areas, each of which may contain hundreds or thousands of control intervals.

Access Methods Services

As I already said, a special utility program called *Access Methods Services* (*IDCAMS*) is used to define the VSAM areas just described. In addition, IDCAMS performs a variety of utility functions such as copying, printing, deleting, and renaming data sets. You'll learn more about using IDCAMS in chapter 3 and throughout the rest of this book. For now, I just want you to remember that IDCAMS must be used to define a VSAM file before a COBOL program may process it.

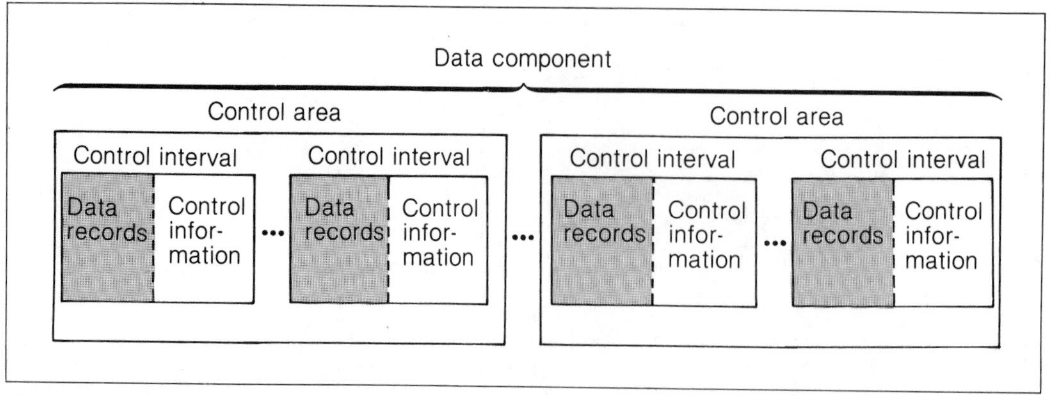

Figure 1-2 VSAM data component structure

The VSAM catalog structure

Unlike standard OS data management, which allows you to maintain files that aren't cataloged, VSAM requires that *all* of its files be cataloged. VSAM maintains its own catalog files; it doesn't use the system data set catalog maintained by OS. A VSAM catalog is one of two types: a *master catalog* or a *user catalog*. Each installation has only one master catalog. The master catalog catalogs all VSAM data sets either directly or indirectly. A VSAM data set is cataloged directly if it is actually referenced by the master catalog. It is cataloged indirectly if the master catalog refers to a user catalog which in turn refers to the data set.

Figure 1-3 illustrates the relationship between the master catalog, user catalogs, and data sets. The master catalog contains entries defining VSAM data sets, non-VSAM data sets, and user catalogs. The user catalogs contain entries for VSAM data sets and non-VSAM data sets.

Under VS1, if a file that is cataloged in a user catalog is referred to in a job step, the user catalog that contains the file's entry must be specified in a JOBCAT or STEPCAT statement. Under VS2 or MVS, this is not necessary. Instead, the user catalog may be specified by the high-level qualifier in the data set name. For example, on an MVS system, a file named MMA.PAYDATA would be cataloged in a user catalog named MMA. If there is no user catalog by that name, the file is cataloged in the master catalog.

When a data space is defined on a direct-access volume, entries are made in the volume's VTOC and in the specified catalog to establish *volume ownership*. Basically, this means that all VSAM files defined on a volume must be cataloged in the catalog that owns the volume. A volume may be owned by either the master catalog or a user catalog, but every volume that contains a VSAM

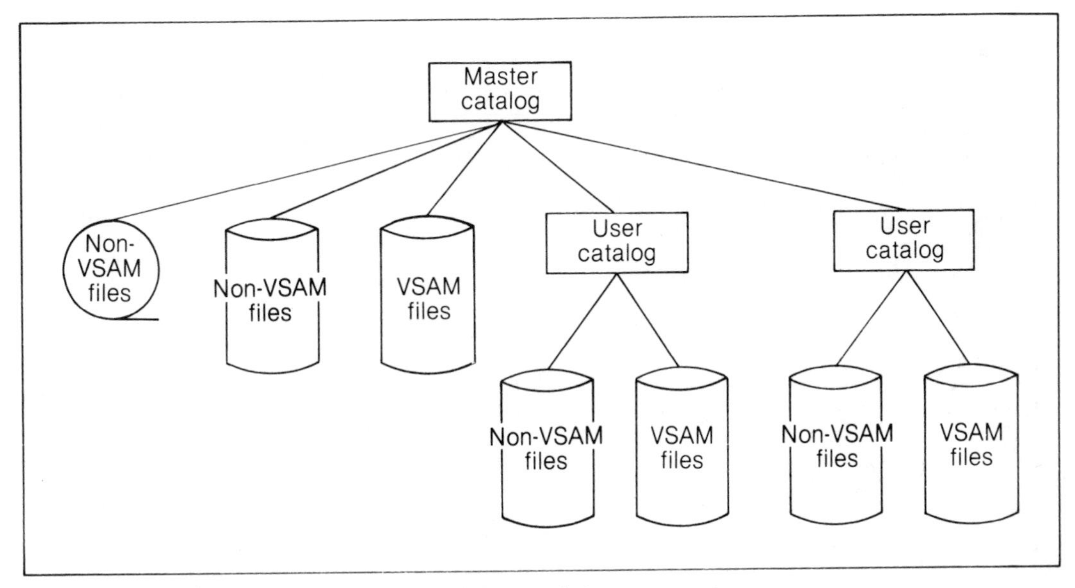

Figure 1-3 Relationship between VSAM catalogs and data sets

file must be owned by a VSAM catalog. Each volume may have only one owner—you can't specify that two catalogs own the same volume. However, a catalog may own more than one volume. The practical result of volume ownership is that all of the VSAM files residing on a disk volume must be cataloged in the same catalog.

Figure 1-4 shows an example of the VSAM catalog structure on an MVS system. In this example, two companies are sharing one computer. To eliminate the possibility of duplicate file names, each company is assigned a user catalog controlling one volume. When I code DSN=GDC.CUSTMSTR, MVS uses the high-level qualifier (GDC) to determine the user catalog. The entry in the user catalog points to the volume and data space containing the data set (in this case, the data set is contained in data space 1 on volume C). As you can see, volume C is owned by GDC and volume B is owned by MMA. Volume A contains the master catalog, some system files, and some files that are common to both users.

Discussion

Quite frankly, many of the concepts presented in this topic are not essential to the COBOL programmer who uses VSAM files. However, I have presented them here because (1) the concepts are useful in understanding the operation of VSAM and (2) the IBM manuals are drenched with this type of terminology. So if you are having trouble understanding some of these concepts, take heart. Go

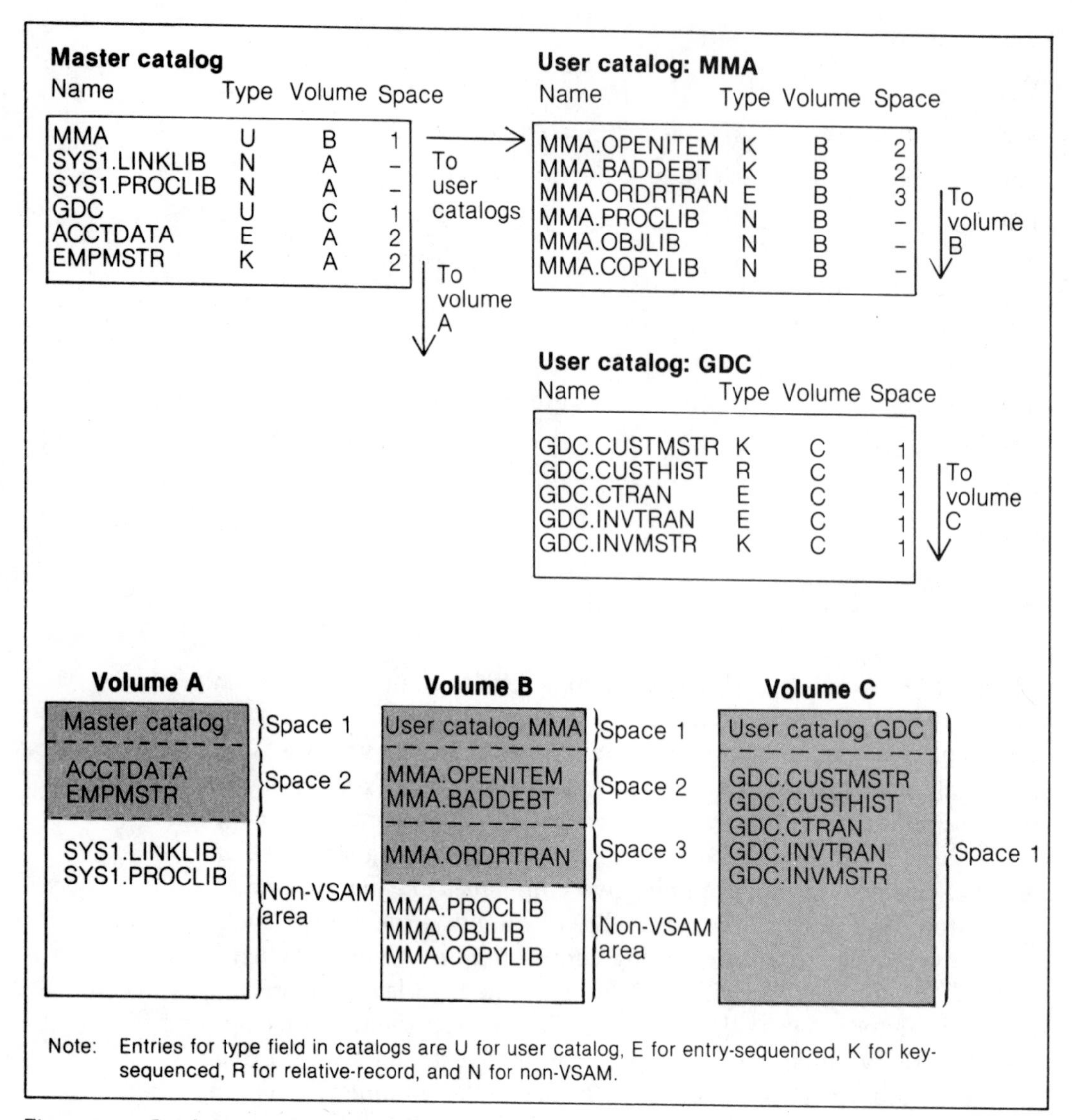

Figure 1-4 Catalog structure on an MVS system

on to chapters 2 and 3. Then, you can reread the portions of this chapter you still don't understand. I think you'll develop a better understanding of the concepts and terminology by seeing them used in context.

Terminology

VSAM
Virtual Storage Access Method
Entry-Sequenced Data Set
ESDS
data set
Key-Sequenced Data Set
KSDS
indexed file
Relative-Record Data Set
RRDS
cluster
data component
data space
control interval
spanned record
control area
Access Methods Services
IDCAMS
master catalog
user catalog
directly cataloged
indirectly cataloged
volume ownership

Objectives

1. Explain the meaning of the following terms:

   key-sequenced data set
   data space
   cluster
   IDCAMS
   master catalog
   user catalog

PART TWO

VSAM Key-Sequenced Files

Probably 95 percent or more of all VSAM files are key-sequenced (indexed). As a result, this part of the book presents what you need to know to process key-sequenced files in COBOL. Chapter 2 presents the language elements necessary to process VSAM key-sequenced files; chapter 3 shows you how to use the VSAM utility program (IDCAMS) to perform basic utility functions for VSAM files. When you complete these chapters, you will be able to develop new COBOL programs for VSAM files as well as to modify existing ISAM programs so they will process VSAM files.

Although the material in this part is specific to OS systems, it is generally applicable to DOS systems. Any variations for DOS users will be mentioned here and discussed in detail in chapter 6.

=(NEW,KEEP),UNIT=3330,VØL=SER=TIRK01,
E=(CYL,(01)),DCB=DSØRG=IS
PGM=IEFBR14
DSN=IMS2.TIRKS.REF.LØCINDDØ,
=(NEW,KEEP),UNIT=3330,VØL=SER=TIRK01,
E=(CYL,(04))
EC PGM=IEFBR14
DSN=IMS2.TIRKS.REF.LØCINDDP,
=(NEW,KEEP),UNIT=3330,VØL=SER=TIRK01,
E=(CYL,(03))
EC PGM=IEFBR14
SD30
/03

2

Processing Key-Sequenced Files

This chapter shows you how to process VSAM key-sequenced files in COBOL. There are three topics in this chapter. Topic 1 presents some conceptual information related to key-sequenced file organization. Topic 2 presents the COBOL elements used to process key-sequenced files. Since VSAM error processing is a complicated subject in itself, topic 3 presents some techniques for handling error conditions in COBOL.

Throughout this chapter, I assume you have a basic understanding of ISAM file processing. If you don't, I recommend you read chapters 8 and 9 of our *Structured ANS COBOL, Part 2,* before you study this chapter.

Although this chapter is geared towards OS users, nearly all the information presented is the same for DOS users. In fact, the only major variation for DOS users is the assignment name in the ASSIGN clause of the SELECT statement for a VSAM file. Refer to chapter 6 for the details of this variation.

TOPIC 1 Key-Sequenced File Concepts

A VSAM *key-sequenced data set* (often called a *KSDS,* or just an *indexed file*) is in many ways similar to an ISAM file. In fact, one of the main reasons IBM developed VSAM was to replace ISAM. As a result, perhaps 95 percent or more of all VSAM files are key-sequenced files. Because of VSAM's improved index structure and overflow handling, VSAM key-sequenced files can be processed more efficiently than ISAM files. For this reason, most users of VS systems should convert their ISAM files to VSAM as soon as they can.

Like ISAM files, VSAM key-sequenced files can be processed in two ways: sequentially or randomly. When *sequential processing* is used, the records are processed one at a time in the order of the key values stored in the file index. When *random processing* is used, the programmer must supply the value of the key for the record that is to be processed.

A key-sequenced cluster consists of two parts: a data component, which contains the actual records of the file, and an *index component*. The index component contains the indexes necessary to access the records in the data component based on a key value. These two components of a VSAM indexed file are illustrated in figure 2-1.

The index component

As you can see in figure 2-1, the index component of a key-sequenced file consists of two parts: a *sequence set* and an *index set*. The sequence set is the lowest level of the index; it is searched to determine which control interval in the data component contains the desired record. The index set is used if the sequence set requires more than one record; it is searched to determine which record of the sequence set indexes the desired record.

To illustrate how this index structure works, consider the key-sequenced file shown in figure 2-2. In this example, the key value represents a five-digit item number in a file of inventory records. The index set contains four entries; each entry contains a pointer to a

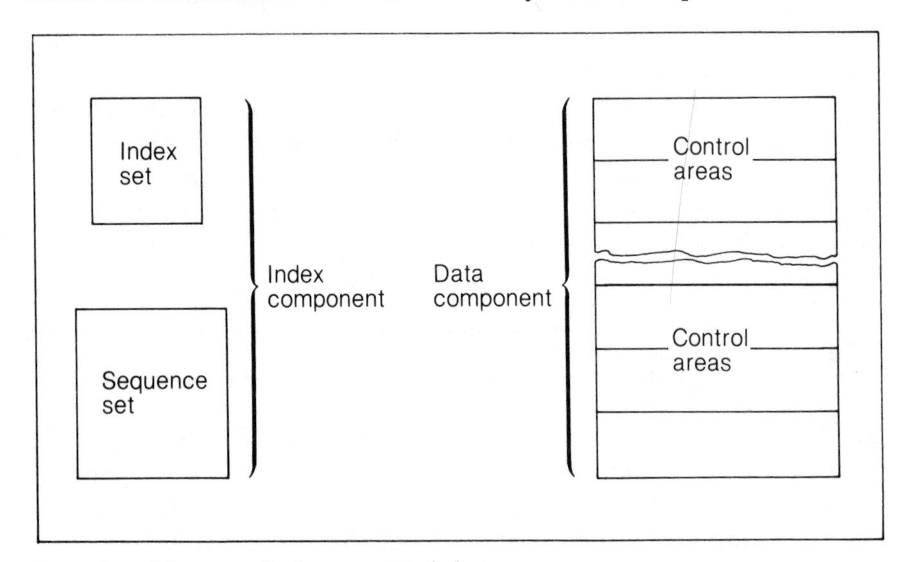

Figure 2-1 Elements of a key-sequenced cluster

Index component				
Index set (level 1)		Sequence set		
Key	Pointer	Record	Key	Pointer
397	S1	1	187	C1
			284	C2
940	S2		322	C3
			397	C4
1391	S3	2	513	C5
1833	S4		641	C6
			787	C7
			940	C8
		3	991	C9
			1205	C10
			1297	C11
			1391	C12
		4	1522	C13
			1639	C14
			1740	C15
			1833	C16

Data component						
Control interval	Keys in control interval					
1	012	041	049	094	101	187
2	188	210	218	247	250	284
3	287	291	294	301	307	322
4	341	348	354	363	370	397
5	410	415	420	434	470	513
6	585	592	601	615	621	641
7	660	680	685	710	740	787
8	812	819	901	914	927	940
9	951	957	967	984	985	991
10	1032	1105	1117	1121	1187	1205
11	1207	1208	1231	1239	1250	1297
12	1330	1337	1341	1355	1366	1391
13	1410	1415	1423	1480	1481	1522
14	1523	1530	1537	1539	1599	1639
15	1641	1645	1691	1701	1703	1740
16	1748	1780	1788	1790	1805	1833

Figure 2-2 Accessing structure of a key-sequenced file

record in the sequence set and the value of the highest key indexed by that record. Similarly, each record of the sequence set contains entries consisting of a pointer to a control interval and the value of the highest key contained in that control interval. In the data component, the records are stored sequentially in each control interval.

Suppose that a program has to find the record with key 1239 in this file. First, the index set would be searched for a key greater than or equal to 1239. Thus, the program would find that the record with key 1239 is indexed in record 3 of the sequence set. Next, record 3 of the sequence set is searched for a high or equal key. This search reveals that key 1239 is contained in control interval 11. Finally, control interval 11 is read and searched sequentially until the desired record is found.

If the index set is very large, it will be divided into multiple levels. In this case, the highest level of the index set is searched, yielding a pointer to the proper record in the next lower level of the index set. This process continues until the lowest level of the index set has been searched. Then the sequence set is searched as usual.

Free space

When a VSAM key-sequenced file is defined, space is reserved to allow for new records. This space can be reserved in two ways: (1) space may be reserved in each control interval, and (2) entire control intervals may be reserved. When you define the data set (using IDCAMS), you specify both types of free space as percentages. For instance, you might specify that 10 percent of the space in each control interval and 15 percent of the control intervals in each control area be reserved for free space.

To illustrate, consider figure 2-3. Here, 25 percent of each control interval and 20 percent of the control intervals in each control area are reserved. As a result, each control interval contains three records and enough room to hold one more, and each control area contains four control intervals for data and one free control interval.

Figure 2-4 shows how the free space within a control interval is used when a record is inserted. In this example, a record with a key value of 6494 is inserted. As you can see, the record is placed after key 6492 and the remaining records in the control interval are moved forward one record position. This movement takes place within VSAM's virtual-storage buffer; the control interval is not rewritten to the disk until its space in the buffer is needed by another control interval. As a result, insertions under VSAM are more efficient than insertions under ISAM.

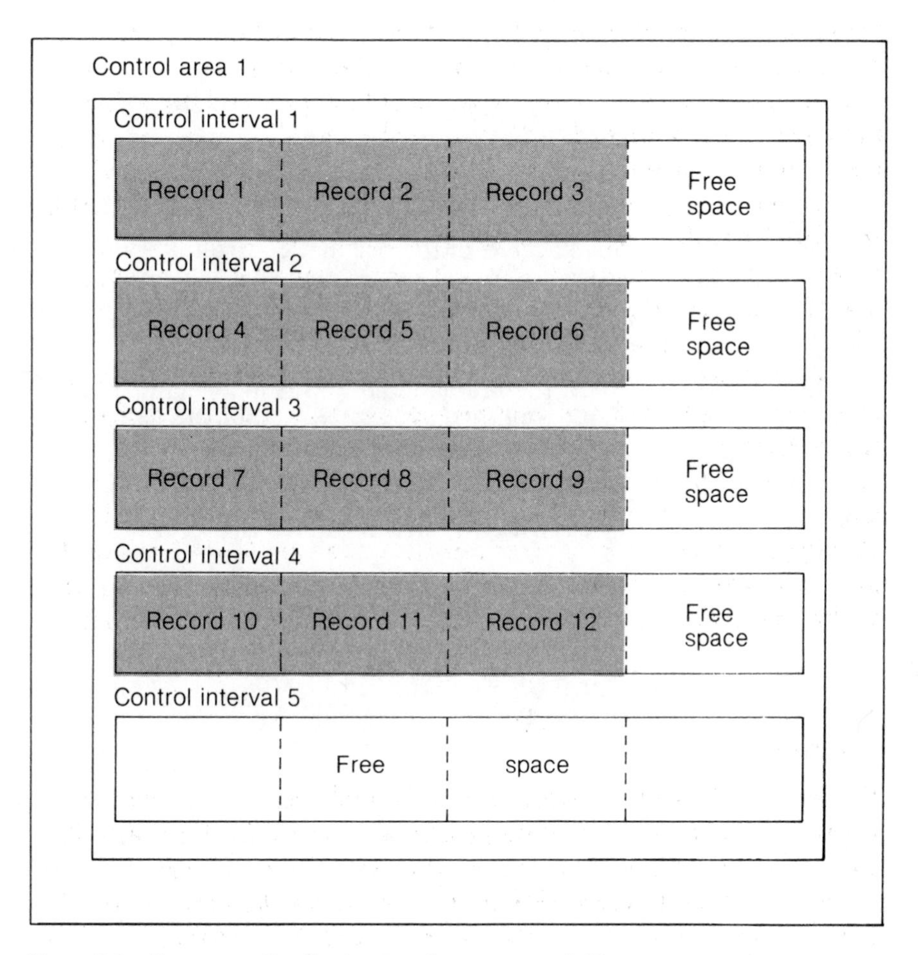

Figure 2-3 Free space distribution in a key-sequenced file

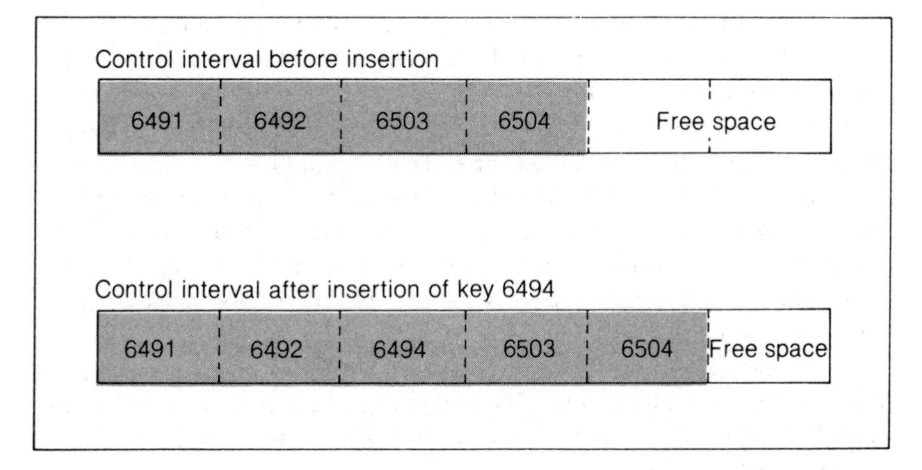

Figure 2-4 Using free space within a control interval to add a record

But what happens if there is no more free space remaining in the control interval? That's where the free control intervals come in. To illustrate, consider figure 2-5. Here, a record with a key value of 6497 is inserted in a control interval that has no free space. In this case, a *control-interval split* occurs: the record is placed after key 6494, and records 6498, 6503, and 6504 are placed in the free control interval. The space thus vacated in the original control interval is made available for further insertions. Again, this movement takes place in the virtual-storage buffer; no disk I-O is done until necessary.

Deletions in a VSAM file are handled in a similar manner. When a record is deleted from a VSAM file, the data is actually removed from the control interval. The space thus vacated becomes immediately available for insertion of a new record. This is a considerable improvement over ISAM, which offered no set way of handling deletions.

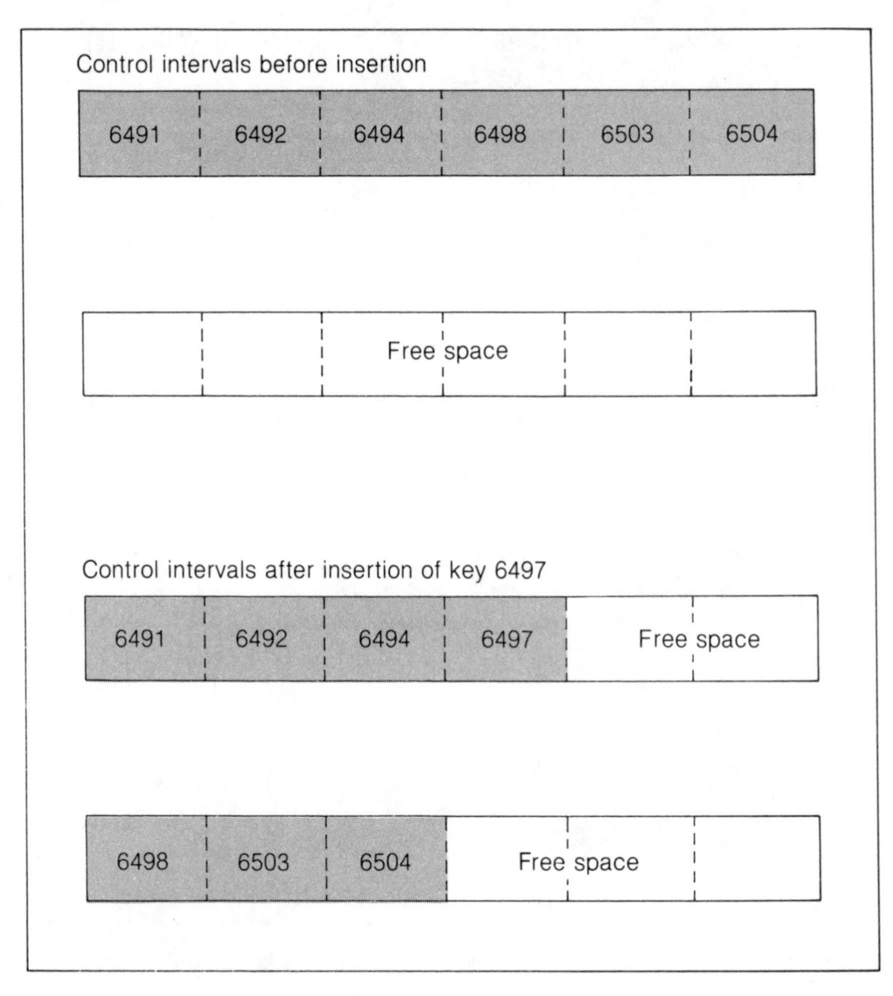

Figure 2-5 A control interval split

JCL for key-sequenced files

As I said in chapter 1, the JCL for VSAM files is very simple. The DD statement for a VSAM file requires only two parameters, DSNAME and DISP, and the DISP parameter is always coded OLD. To illustrate, consider this DD statement:

```
//INVMSTR DD DSN=H4$.INVMSTR,
//           DISP=OLD
```

Here, the file named H4$.INVMSTR has already been defined by the IDCAMS utility. This same DD statement can be used for every COBOL program that processes the file, whether it's a file-creation program or an update program.

The ISAM interface program

It is possible to process a VSAM file with a program designed for an ISAM file. This is done by means of a special *ISAM interface program* supplied by IBM. The ISAM interface program intercepts all ISAM requests and translates them into VSAM requests. To invoke the ISAM interface, you simply code AMP=AMORG on the DD statement for the VSAM file.

Figure 2-6 shows a job step that uses an ISAM file and the same job step after the ISAM file has been converted to a VSAM key-sequenced file. Since the same program is used unchanged to access the VSAM file, the ddname of this file must be exactly the same in both steps. In this example, the ddname is FORTAB. The DSN is different, though, because the file was given a new data set name when

A job step to process an ISAM file

```
//UPSTEP    EXEC  PGM=UPDMAST
//FORIPT    DD  DSN=FORMIN,
//              DISP=OLD
//FORTAB    DD  DSN=FORMTBLE,
//              DISP=OLD,
//              DCB=DSORG=IS
//FORLST    DD  SYSOUT=A
```

A job step executing the same program to process a VSAM file

```
//UPSTEP    EXEC  PGM=UPDMAST
//FORIPT    DD  DSN=FORMIN,
//              DISP=OLD
//FORTAB    DD  DSN=FORMTAB,
//              DISP=OLD,
//              AMP=AMORG
//FORLST    DD  SYSOUT=A
```

Figure 2-6 JCL for using the ISAM interface program

it was converted to a VSAM file. The AMP=AMORG parameter is coded to tell OS/VS that the file is a VSAM file even though the program is coded to process an ISAM file. This combination automatically causes the ISAM interface program to be invoked.

In some respects, the ISAM interface is an unfortunate thing. IBM developed it to encourage conversion to VSAM by allowing users to gradually convert their ISAM programs. Most installations, however, feel that the conversion effort is done once the JCL has been modified to invoke the ISAM interface. And so they never modify their ISAM programs.

However, there is a good reason why you should modify your programs to process VSAM files, even though the ISAM interface seems to be working fine. As I mentioned earlier, ISAM offers no set way to handle deletions. So ISAM programs must use special coding techniques to handle deleted records. Usually, to delete a record, HIGH-VALUE is moved to the first byte of the record and the record is rewritten to indicate that it has been deleted. The records are not actually removed from the file until it is reorganized. As a result, programs that process the file must look for a delete-code in the first byte to see if the record is active. Unfortunately, VSAM doesn't recognize this record-deletion scheme, so you have the same problem with VSAM that you had with ISAM—the file soon becomes full of inactive records and must be reorganized. But how do you reorganize a VSAM file? You must write a program yourself to remove the records that have a delete-code in the first byte—there is no IBM-supplied utility to remove these records.

So if you're going to use the ISAM interface, remember that it is meant to be a temporary solution to the conversion problem. Eventually, and the sooner the better, you should modify your ISAM programs so they handle VSAM files directly, without using the ISAM interface. Then, VSAM will handle deletions in a way that makes the space available for file additions so reorganization is unnecessary.

Terminology

key-sequenced data set
KSDS
indexed file
sequential processing
random processing
index component
sequence set
index set
control interval split
ISAM interface program

Objectives

1. Explain the differences between ISAM and VSAM indexed file organization.
2. Given reference material, code a DD statement for a VSAM file.
3. Explain the use of the ISAM interface.

Problems

1. Suppose you have written a COBOL program that processes a VSAM file named H4$.GMAST.PAYROLL. Code an acceptable DD statement to define this file. The file's ddname is PAYMAST.

Solutions

1. Here is an acceptable DD statement:

```
//PAYMAST  DD  DSN=H4$.GMAST.PAYROLL,
//               DISP=OLD
```

TOPIC 2 COBOL for Key-Sequenced Files

This topic presents the COBOL elements required to process a VSAM indexed file. When IBM originally developed ISAM, the ANSI COBOL standards (1968) did not provide for indexed file handling. As a result, IBM added extensions to the standard COBOL language. These extensions are the language elements you are familiar with for processing ISAM files.

By the time IBM announced VSAM, however, the 1974 COBOL standards had been adopted. The 1974 standards do provide for indexed files, and IBM's VS COBOL compilers support these standards for VSAM files. Although there are many similarities between the 1968 ISAM extensions and the 1974 standards, there are also many differences.

As a result, converting an ISAM program to VSAM really means converting a 1968 standard COBOL program to the 1974 standards. In effect, then, this topic presents the 1974 language elements as they are used to process VSAM files. Remember that these elements are not supported by older versions of IBM's COBOL compiler; you must be using the VS compiler to process VSAM files using these language elements.

A word about the VS COBOL compiler before I go on. A compile-time option (LANGLVL) is used to specify which COBOL

```
IDENTIFICATION DIVISION.
     .
     .
ENVIRONMENT DIVISION.
     .
     .
INPUT-OUTPUT SECTION.
FILE-CONTROL.
    SELECT file-name ASSIGN TO assignment-name
                     ORGANIZATION IS INDEXED
                     ACCESS MODE IS SEQUENTIAL
                     RECORD KEY IS data-name
                     FILE STATUS IS data-name.
```

Note: The NOMINAL KEY field is not used for VSAM files.

```
     .
     .
DATA DIVISION.
FILE SECTION.
FD   file-name
     LABEL RECORDS ARE STANDARD
     RECORD CONTAINS integer CHARACTERS.
```

Notes: 1. The RECORD KEY field must be described in the File Section as a field within the disk record.
2. The RECORDING MODE clause is invalid for VSAM files.
3. The BLOCK CONTAINS clause is optional for VSAM files and should not be coded.

Figure 2-7 COBOL elements for processing key-sequenced files sequentially (part 1 of 2)

standard is in effect. If LANGLVL=1 is specified, the program is compiled according to the 1968 standards; if LANGLVL=2 is specified, the 1974 standards are used. However, this option only affects the few COBOL elements that have different meanings for the two standards. The VSAM language elements presented in this topic will function the same no matter how this option is set. Similarly, the 1968 ISAM language extensions may be used no matter how the LANGLVL option is set.

There are two methods for processing VSAM indexed files: sequential and random. When sequential processing is used, the records are automatically accessed in key sequence. When random processing is used, you must specify a key value for each access; the records are retrieved in no particular sequence.

SEQUENTIAL PROCESSING

Figure 2-7 summarizes the COBOL elements for processing VSAM key-sequenced files sequentially. These elements are essentially the same as those used for ISAM files. However, there are a few important variations. These differences are shaded in figure 2-7.

```
PROCEDURE DIVISION.
     .
     .
           (INPUT   file-name ...)
     OPEN  {OUTPUT  file-name ...}      ...
           (I-O     file-name ...)

                                   (EQUAL TO        )
                                   (=               )
     START file-name [KEY IS      {GREATER THAN     }  data-name]
                                   (>               )
                                   (NOT LESS THAN   )
                                   (NOT <           )

               [INVALID KEY imperative-statement].

     READ file-name RECORD
          [INTO data-name]
          [AT END imperative-statement].

     WRITE record-name
          [FROM data-name]
          [INVALID KEY imperative-statement].

     REWRITE record-name
          [FROM data-name]
          [INVALID KEY imperative-statement].

     DELETE file-name RECORD
          [INVALID KEY imperative-statement].

     CLOSE file-name ...
```

Figure 2-7 COBOL elements for processing key-sequenced files sequentially (part 2 of 2)

The Environment Division

The SELECT statement The assigment name used in the ASSIGN clause of the SELECT statement for a key-sequenced VSAM file uses a different format than the one used for an ISAM file. The VSAM format is this:

```
comment-ddname
```

In the sample programs in this topic, I have omitted the comment so the assignment name is simply the ddname that is used in the JCL for the program. (Under DOS VSAM, the assignment name's format is somewhat different. See chapter 6 for details.)

You must specify ORGANIZATION IS INDEXED in the SELECT statement for a key-sequenced file (under ISAM, the organization is specified in the ASSIGN clause). Then, you use the ACCESS MODE clause to specify that the file will be processed sequentially. Although this clause can be omitted (sequential processing will be assumed), it is usually included because it is good documentation. The combination of the ORGANIZATION and ACCESS clauses makes it clear that the file has indexed organization but is accessed sequentially.

The RECORD KEY clause gives the data name of the control field in the records of the file. This is the field that is used in the cluster's index component so the correct record can be located. When processing an inventory file, for example, the RECORD KEY is normally the item number. This field must actually be within the disk record in the File Section; it can't be a separate field in working storage.

Notice that there is no NOMINAL KEY clause in the SELECT statement for a VSAM file. Under ISAM, the NOMINAL KEY clause specifies a field defined in working storage that is used to access the records in the file. Under VSAM, the function of the NOMINAL KEY field is handled by the RECORD KEY field.

The FILE STATUS clause specifies a field that is updated by the system after each I/O statement for the file is executed. The FILE STATUS field must be defined in working storage, and its PICTURE should be XX. When an error condition occurs, the system puts a two-digit error code in the FILE STATUS field. Then, the program can examine the code to determine the nature of the error and decide what action should be taken.

Figure 2-8 summarizes the FILE STATUS error codes that are most often encountered when processing VSAM indexed files. The first code, 00, indicates that no error has occurred. The next code, 10, means the end of the file has been reached—in other words, the AT END condition has occurred. The next three codes correspond to the INVALID KEY conditions for ISAM files: code 21 means an out-of-sequence record has been found during sequential processing, code 22 means that you tried to write a record with a duplicate key, and code 23 means that you tried to read a record that doesn't exist. The last code, 24, is used to indicate that no more space is available for the file. You'll see how these codes are used in the programming examples in this topic. And in the next topic, you'll learn more about processing these error conditions as well as other, less common, conditions.

The Data Division

In the Data Division, the disk records in a key-sequenced file are defined as they are for any file organization. The FD statement for a key-sequenced file is much the same as for an ISAM file. However, there are three important differences. First, the LABEL RECORDS clause, though always required, is treated as documentation no mat-

FILE STATUS

Value	Meaning
00	Successful completion
10	End of file reached
21	Sequence error
22	Duplicate key
23	Record not found
24	No more space

Figure 2-8 FILE STATUS values for common I/O errors that occur when using key-sequenced files

ter how you code it. Second, the RECORDING MODE clause is not allowed. Third, the BLOCK CONTAINS clause is optional for VSAM and is usually omitted.

Like ISAM, VSAM requires that the record key field in a key-sequenced record be defined in the File Section. As a result, although you can still use the INTO and FROM options of the READ and WRITE statements for a key-sequenced file, the key field must be defined in the File Section. In a case like this, you will define the entire record in the Working-Storage Section and just the key field in the File Section.

The Procedure Division

The Procedure Division statements for sequential processing of a key-sequenced file are much the same as those for an ISAM file. However, there are a few variations.

To begin with, the START statement has an extended format. Instead of placing a starting value in the NOMINAL KEY field, the starting key is placed in the field specified by the RECORD KEY clause of the SELECT statement. Then, the KEY clause of the START statement (a new feature) can be used to establish the first record to be processed in the file. If the KEY clause is omitted, processing starts with the key equal to the RECORD KEY field. If the record doesn't exist, an error results. Because it's convenient to be able to start processing at the first record equal to or greater than a certain value, you might use the START statement like this:

```
MOVE 1000 TO IM-ITEM-NO.
START INVMSTR
    KEY IS NOT LESS THAN IM-ITEM-NO.
```

In this case, processing would begin with key 1000. If there were no record with key 1000, processing would start with the first record with a key greater than 1000. When the START statement isn't used, processing begins with the first record in the file.

The DELETE statement—not available for ISAM—is used to delete records from a VSAM file. When used in the sequential access mode, it deletes the record that was read by the last READ statement. To use the DELETE statement, the file must be opened as I-O. The DELETE statement causes the records to actually be deleted from the file, so the space is immediately made available for new records. Under ISAM, remember, deleted records aren't removed from the file until the file is reorganized.

The INVALID KEY clause—used on the WRITE, REWRITE, START, and DELETE statements—is always optional. When using sequential processing, the statement specified in the INVALID KEY clause is executed if one of four conditions occurs: (1) you try to write a record with a duplicate key, (2) you try to write a record that is out of sequence, (3) you try to read a record that doesn't exist, or (4) you try to write beyond the space allocated for the file. As you can see in figure 2-8, all of these conditions have a FILE STATUS value whose first digit is 2.

I recommend you always omit the INVALID KEY clause. Instead, follow each I/O statement with IF statements that test the FILE STATUS field and perform the necessary action based on the error code. This technique is better because it catches all error conditions—not just the INVALID KEY conditions. You will see this technique used in the programing examples in this topic. And in the next topic, I will discuss VSAM error handling in detail.

Program example: a file creation program

Creating a key-sequenced file is much like creating an ISAM file. Usually, a non-VSAM sequential or ISAM input file provides the data that goes into each VSAM record. Since the indexed records must be written in key sequence, the input records must also be in key sequence.

Figures 2-9 and 2-10 present a simple program that creates a file of inventory records from a standard sequential file. The records are 32 bytes long and contain these fields: item number (the key field that is specified in the RECORD KEY clause of the SELECT statement), item description, on-hand balance (a COMP-3 field that will require only three bytes of actual storage), and four FILLER bytes. As you can see in the structure chart in figure 2-9, the main processing module, module 100, reads an input record and writes it on the output file. The complete listing for this program is given in figure 2-10. The shaded portions of figure 2-10 indicate the coding elements unique to VSAM.

The SELECT statement for the new inventory master file, INV-MSTR, includes all of the clauses shown in figure 2-7. After the ASSIGN clause, the ORGANIZATION and ACCESS clauses show

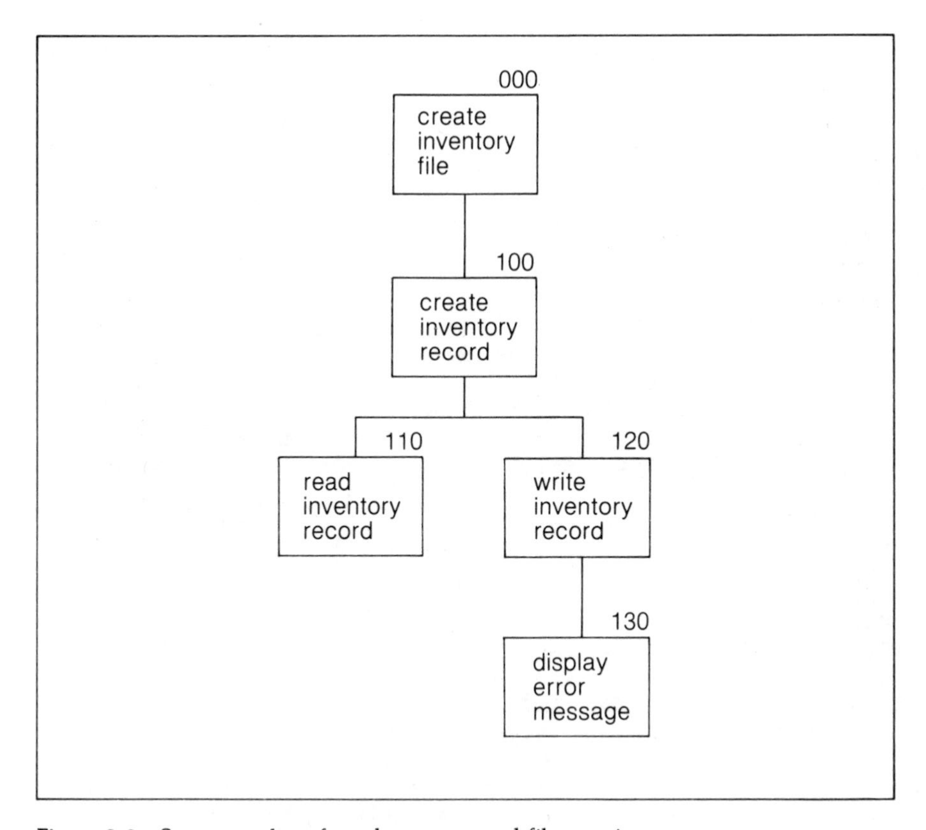

Figure 2-9 Structure chart for a key-sequenced file-creation program

that this is an indexed file that will be processed sequentially. The RECORD KEY field is IM-ITEM-NUMBER, and a FILE STATUS field, INVMSTR-ERROR-CODE, is specified for error processing.

After the WRITE statement in module 120, an IF statement tests the FILE STATUS field and performs module 130 if it isn't zero. This module, in turn, uses the FILE STATUS field to determine the cause of any I/O errors. If the FILE STATUS field is zero, there is no error, so processing continues. If the FILE STATUS is equal to 21, it indicates an out-of-sequence record, so an appropriate message is printed using a DISPLAY statement. If the error code is 22, it means a duplicate record key was detected, and an error message is displayed. In either case, the transaction record in error is ignored and processing continues. If the error code is not 21 or 22, it means some other, more serious type of error occurred. So a DISPLAY statement is used to print an error message along with the value of the FILE STATUS field, and INVCARDS-EOF-SW is turned on to cause the program to end. Then, the programmer can look up the error code in a reference manual to determine the cause of the problem. In the next topic, you will learn more about VSAM error handling.

```
 IDENTIFICATION DIVISION.
*
 PROGRAM-ID.  VSKCR.
*
 ENVIRONMENT DIVISION.
*
 INPUT-OUTPUT SECTION.
*
 FILE-CONTROL.
     SELECT INVCARDS ASSIGN TO UT-S-INVCARDS.
     SELECT INVMSTR  ASSIGN TO INVMSTR
                     ORGANIZATION IS INDEXED
                     ACCESS IS SEQUENTIAL
                     RECORD KEY IS IM-ITEM-NUMBER
                     FILE STATUS IS INVMSTR-ERROR-CODE.
*
 DATA DIVISION.
*
 FILE SECTION.
*
 FD  INVCARDS
     LABEL RECORDS ARE STANDARD
     RECORDING MODE IS F
     RECORD CONTAINS 80 CHARACTERS
     BLOCK CONTAINS 0 RECORDS.
*
 01  IC-AREA                 PIC X(80).
*
 FD  INVMSTR
     LABEL RECORDS ARE STANDARD
     RECORD CONTAINS 32 CHARACTERS.
*
 01  IM-RECORD.
*
     05  IM-ITEM-NUMBER  PIC X(5).
     05  IM-ITEM-DESC    PIC X(20).
     05  IM-ON-HAND      PIC S9(5)    COMP-3.
     05  FILLER          PIC X(4).
*
 WORKING-STORAGE SECTION.
*
 01  SWITCHES.
*
     05  INVCARDS-EOF-SW      PIC X    VALUE 'N'.
         88  INVCARDS-EOF              VALUE 'Y'.
*
 01  FILE-STATUS-FIELD.
*
     05  INVMSTR-ERROR-CODE  PIC XX.
*
 01  IC-RECORD.
*
```

Figure 2-10 Program listing for a key-sequenced file-creation program (part 1 of 2)

```
           05  IC-ITEM-NUMBER  PIC X(5).
           05  IC-ITEM-DESC    PIC X(20).
           05  IC-ON-HAND      PIC 9(5).
           05  FILLER          PIC X(50).
      *
       PROCEDURE DIVISION.
      *
       000-CREATE-INVENTORY-FILE.
      *
           OPEN INPUT  INVCARDS
                OUTPUT INVMSTR.
           PERFORM 100-CREATE-INVENTORY-RECORD
               UNTIL INVCARDS-EOF.
           CLOSE INVCARDS
                 INVMSTR.
           DISPLAY 'VSKCR  I  1  NORMAL EOJ'.
           STOP RUN.
      *
       100-CREATE-INVENTORY-RECORD.
      *
           PERFORM 110-READ-INVENTORY-RECORD.
           IF NOT INVCARDS-EOF
               MOVE IC-ITEM-NUMBER TO IM-ITEM-NUMBER
               MOVE IC-ITEM-DESC   TO IM-ITEM-DESC
               MOVE IC-ON-HAND     TO IM-ON-HAND
               PERFORM 120-WRITE-INVENTORY-RECORD.
      *
       110-READ-INVENTORY-RECORD.
      *
           READ INVCARDS INTO IC-RECORD
               AT END
                   MOVE 'Y' TO INVCARDS-EOF-SW.
      *
       120-WRITE-INVENTORY-RECORD.
      *
           WRITE IM-RECORD.
           IF INVMSTR-ERROR-CODE NOT = 00
               PERFORM 130-DISPLAY-ERROR-MESSAGE.
      *
       130-DISPLAY-ERROR-MESSAGE.
      *
           IF INVMSTR-ERROR-CODE = 21
               DISPLAY 'VSKCR  A  2  OUT OF SEQ RECORD--ITEM NO '
                       IM-ITEM-NUMBER '.'
           ELSE IF INVMSTR-ERROR-CODE = 22
               DISPLAY 'VSKCR  A  3  DUPLICATE KEY FOR ITEM NO '
                       IM-ITEM-NUMBER '.'
           ELSE
               DISPLAY 'VSKCR  A  4  WRITE ERROR FOR ITEM NO '
                       IM-ITEM-NUMBER
                       '.  FILE STATUS ' INVMSTR-ERROR-CODE '.'
               MOVE 'Y' TO INVCARDS-EOF-SW.
```

Figure 2-10 Program listing for a key-sequenced file-creation program (part 2 of 2)

Related file-creation tasks I'm sure you realize that you won't often get a chance to write a program as limited as the one in figure 2-10. In fact, IDCAMS (the VSAM utility program) can perform the same function as this program using only a few control statements. In actual practice, a key-sequenced file-creation program will usually edit the input records for valid data and then sort the good input records into key-field sequence before writing them on the VSAM file. However, the coding for these tasks is the same whether the output file is a key-sequenced file or an ISAM file.

Program example: a sequential update program

When updating a key-sequenced file on a sequential basis, processing takes place just as if the file had ISAM organization. The READ statement presents the records to the program one at a time in the order of the RECORD KEY field. When the REWRITE statement is executed, a record is written in the location from which it was originally read.

To illustrate, consider the inventory master file update program described in figure 2-11. As you can see by the system flowchart, there is one input file—a transaction file—and two output files—an update listing and an error file of unmatched transactions (transactions that have no corresponding master record). The inventory master file will be updated in place on the disk.

Figure 2-12 is a structure chart for this program. As you can see, module 100 is the main control module. It controls the reading of the transaction and master files and determines what update action to take based on a comparison of the control fields in the transaction and master records.

The complete listing for this program is given in figure 2-13. The SELECT and FD statements for the inventory file (INVMSTR) are exactly the same as those in the file-creation program. In the Procedure Division, the file is opened as I-O. This means the REWRITE statement will be used to update the records in their original location on the disk.

In module 100, a complex nested IF statement is used to determine the update action after the necessary transaction and master records are read. If the item numbers in the transaction and master records are the same, then the master record is changed, a report line is printed, MASTER-UPDATED-SW is turned on, and NEED-TRANSACTION-SW is set so a new transaction will be read the next time module 100 is executed. If the transaction is greater than the master and MASTER-UPDATED-SW indicates the record was

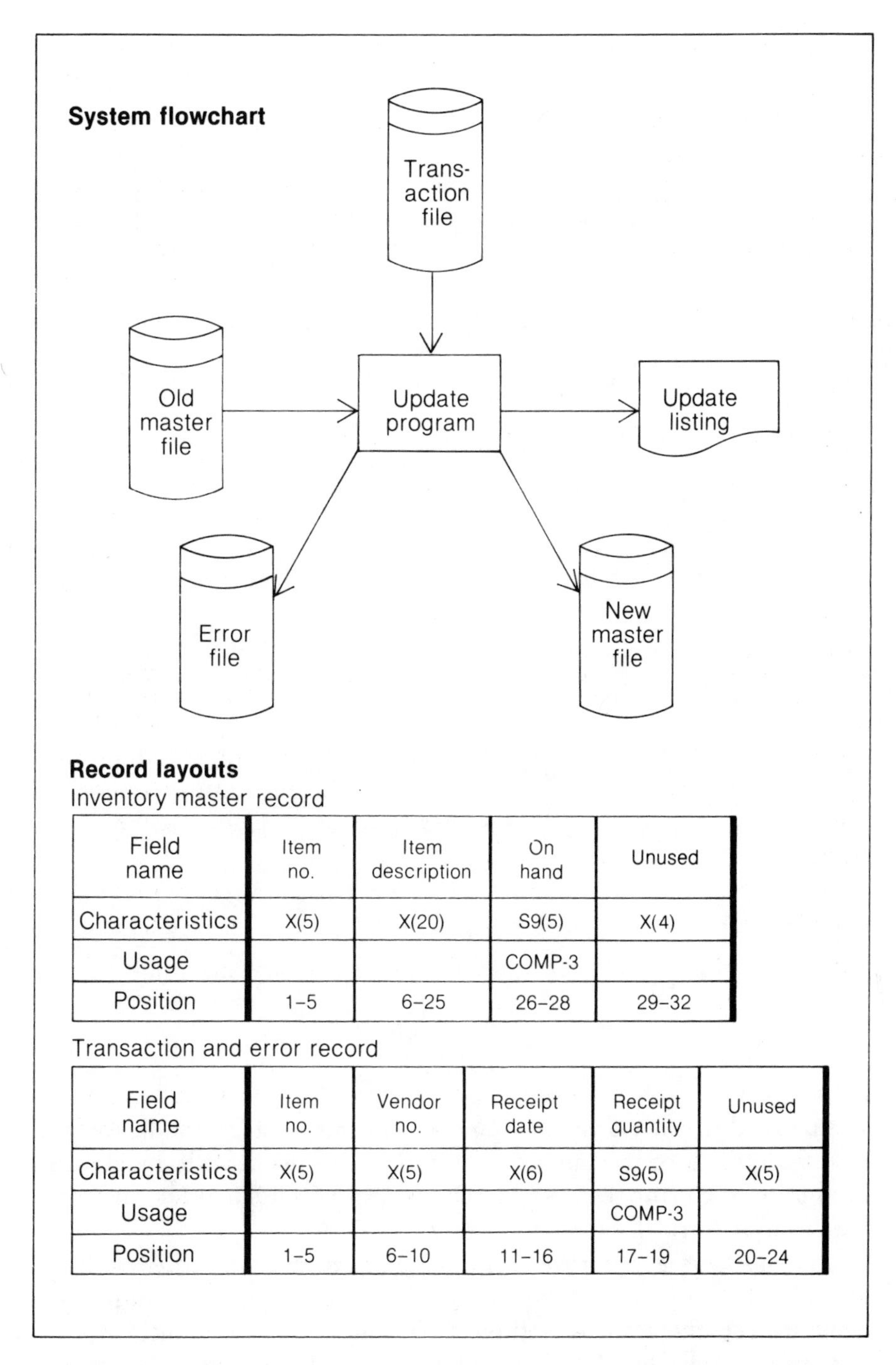

Inventory master record

Field name	Item no.	Item description	On hand	Unused
Characteristics	X(5)	X(20)	S9(5)	X(4)
Usage			COMP-3	
Position	1-5	6-25	26-28	29-32

Transaction and error record

Field name	Item no.	Vendor no.	Receipt date	Receipt quantity	Unused
Characteristics	X(5)	X(5)	X(6)	S9(5)	X(5)
Usage				COMP-3	
Position	1-5	6-10	11-16	17-19	20-24

Figure 2-11 Specifications for a sequential update program using a key-sequenced master file (part 1 of 2)

changed, the master record is rewritten. Then, whether the master is rewritten or not, NEED-MASTER-SW is set so a new master record

Print chart

Record Name	Line	Print positions 1–44
	1	
HDG-LINE-1	2	ITEM VENDOR RECEIPT RECEIPT
HDG-LINE-2	3	NO. NO. DATE AMOUNT
NEXT-REPORT-LINE	4	XXXXX XXXXX XX XX XX 99999
	5	XXXXX XXXXX XX XX XX 99999
	6	
	7	
TOTAL-LINE-1	8	99,999 TRANSACTIONS PROCESSED
TOTAL-LINE-2	9	99,999 UNMATCHED TRANSACTIONS
	10	
	11	
	12	VSKSUPD I 1 NORMAL EOJ
	13	
	14	
	15	
	16	
	17	
	18	

Narrative

1. Use transaction records to update master records by adding the receipt amount in the transaction record to the on-hand amount in the master record. There may be none, one, or several transactions for each master, and both files are in item-number sequence.
2. Print an update report with one line for each valid transaction record showing item number, vendor number, receipt date, and receipt quantity.
3. Write a record on the error file if an unmatched transaction is detected.
4. At the end of the report, print total lines showing the number of transactions processed and the number of unmatched transactions.

Figure 2-11 Specifications for a sequential update program using a key-sequenced master file (part 2 of 2)

will be read. If the transaction is less than the master, it indicates an out-of-sequence or unmatched transaction. In this case, the record is written on the error file and NEED-TRANSACTION-SW is set so a new transaction will be read.

If you have ever written an update program for an ISAM file, this VSAM key-sequenced update program should present no problems. In fact, there are only three differences. First, the SELECT statement for the VSAM file is different. Second, the RECORDING MODE and BLOCK CONTAINS clauses of the FD statement are omitted. And third, the FILE STATUS field is examined in an IF statement following each I/O statement to determine if an I/O error has occurred.

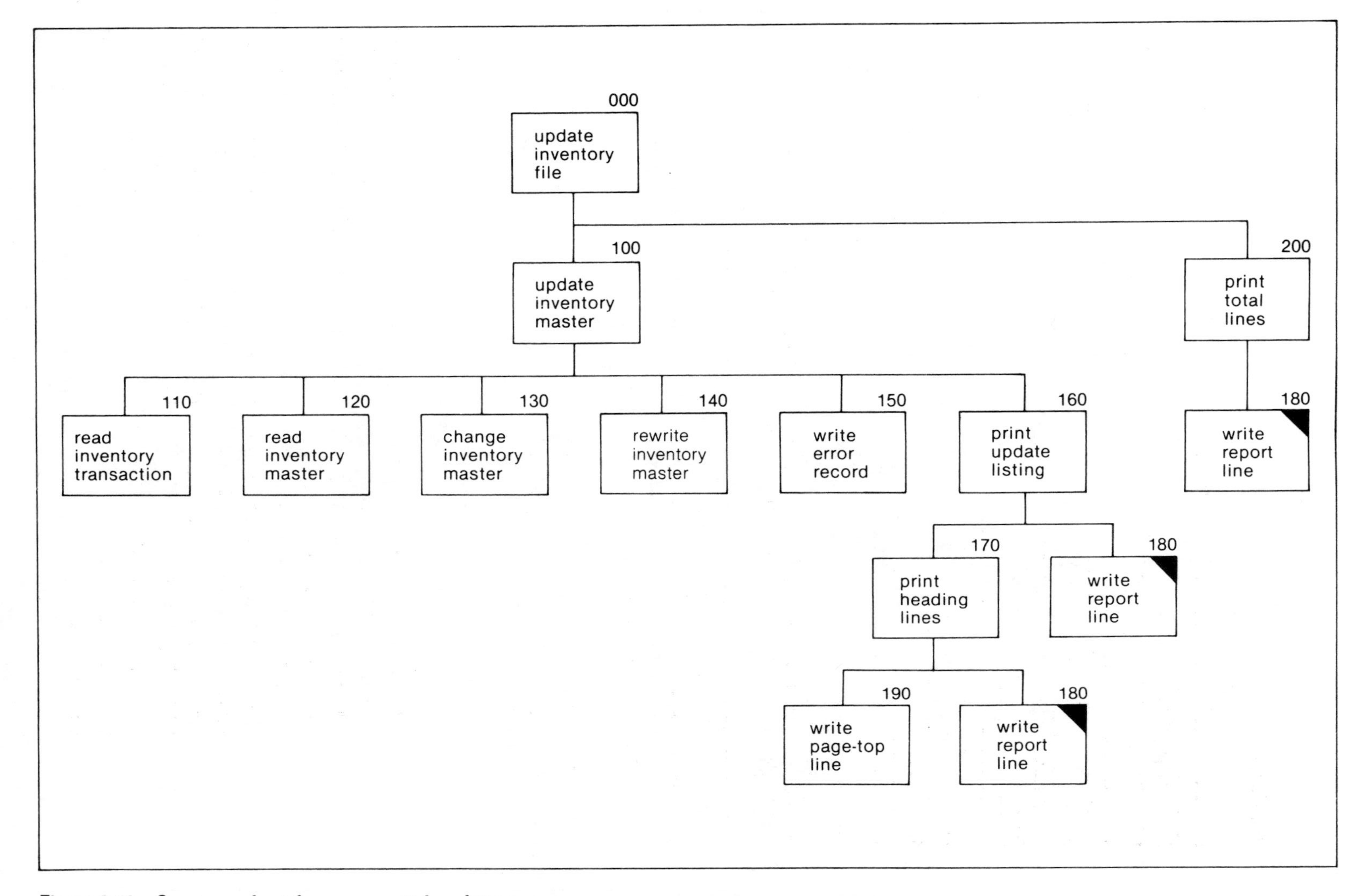

Figure 2-12 Structure chart for a sequential update program

```
 IDENTIFICATION DIVISION.
*
 PROGRAM-ID.  VSKSUPDT.
*
 ENVIRONMENT DIVISION.
*
 CONFIGURATION SECTION.
*
 SPECIAL-NAMES.
     C01 IS PAGE-TOP.
*
 INPUT-OUTPUT SECTION.
*
 FILE-CONTROL.
     SELECT TRANFILE ASSIGN TO UT-S-TRANFILE.
     SELECT INVMSTR  ASSIGN TO INVMSTR
                     ORGANIZATION IS INDEXED
                     ACCESS IS SEQUENTIAL
                     RECORD KEY IS IM-ITEM-NUMBER
                     FILE STATUS IS INVMSTR-ERROR-CODE.
     SELECT ERRFILE  ASSIGN TO UT-S-ERRFILE.
     SELECT UPDLIST  ASSIGN TO UT-S-UPDLIST.
*
 DATA DIVISION.
*
 FILE SECTION.
*
 FD  TRANFILE
     LABEL RECORDS ARE STANDARD
     RECORDING MODE IS F
     RECORD CONTAINS 24 CHARACTERS
     BLOCK CONTAINS 0 RECORDS.
*
 01  TR-AREA                 PIC X(24).
*
 FD  INVMSTR
     LABEL RECORDS ARE STANDARD
     RECORD CONTAINS 32 CHARACTERS.
*
 01  IM-RECORD.
*
     05  IM-ITEM-NUMBER        PIC X(5).
     05  IM-ITEM-DESC          PIC X(20).
     05  IM-ON-HAND            PIC S9(5)        COMP-3.
     05  FILLER                PIC X(4).
*
 FD  ERRFILE
     LABEL RECORDS ARE STANDARD
     RECORDING MODE IS F
     RECORD CONTAINS 24 CHARACTERS
     BLOCK CONTAINS 0 RECORDS.
```

Figure 2-13 Program listing for a sequential update program using a key-sequenced master file (part 1 of 6)

```
*
 01   ER-RECORD              PIC X(24).
*
 FD   UPDLIST
      LABEL RECORDS ARE OMITTED
      RECORDING MODE IS F
      RECORD CONTAINS 133 CHARACTERS
      BLOCK CONTAINS 0 RECORDS.
*
 01   PRINT-AREA             PIC X(133).
*
 WORKING-STORAGE SECTION.
*
 01   SWITCHES.
*
      05   TRAN-EOF-SW                    PIC X     VALUE 'N'.
           88   TRAN-EOF                            VALUE 'Y'.
      05   NEED-TRANSACTION-SW            PIC X     VALUE 'Y'.
           88   NEED-TRANSACTION                    VALUE 'Y'.
      05   NEED-MASTER-SW                 PIC X     VALUE 'Y'.
           88   NEED-MASTER                         VALUE 'Y'.
      05   MASTER-UPDATED-SW              PIC X     VALUE 'N'.
           88   MASTER-UPDATED                      VALUE 'Y'.
*
 01   FILE-STATUS-FIELD.
*
      05   INVMSTR-ERROR-CODE       PIC XX.
*
 01   COUNT-FIELDS                  COMP-3.
*
      05   TRANS-PROCESSED-COUNT    PIC S9(5)       VALUE ZERO.
      05   UNMATCHED-TRANS-COUNT    PIC S9(5)       VALUE ZERO.
*
 01   PRINT-FIELDS                  COMP            SYNC.
*
      05   LINE-COUNT               PIC S99         VALUE +99.
      05   LINES-ON-PAGE            PIC S99         VALUE +57.
      05   SPACE-CONTROL            PIC S9.
*
 01   TR-RECORD.
*
      05   TR-ITEM-NUMBER           PIC X(5).
      05   TR-VENDOR-NUMBER         PIC X(5).
      05   TR-RECEIPT-DATE          PIC X(6).
      05   TR-RECEIPT-QUANTITY      PIC S9(5)       COMP-3.
      05   FILLER                   PIC X(5).
*
 01   HDG-LINE-1.
*
      05   HDG1-CC             PIC X.
      05   FILLER              PIC X(1)     VALUE SPACE.
```

Figure 2-13 Program listing for a sequential update program using a key-sequenced master file (part 2 of 6)

```
           05   FILLER              PIC X(4)     VALUE 'ITEM'.
           05   FILLER              PIC X(2)     VALUE SPACE.
           05   FILLER              PIC X(6)     VALUE 'VENDOR'.
           05   FILLER              PIC X(4)     VALUE SPACE.
           05   FILLER              PIC X(7)     VALUE 'RECEIPT'.
           05   FILLER              PIC X(2)     VALUE SPACE.
           05   FILLER              PIC X(7)     VALUE 'RECEIPT'.
           05   FILLER              PIC X(99)    VALUE SPACE.
      *
       01  HDG-LINE-2.
      *
           05   HDG2-CC             PIC X.
           05   FILLER              PIC X(2)     VALUE SPACE.
           05   FILLER              PIC X(3)     VALUE 'NO.'.
           05   FILLER              PIC X(4)     VALUE SPACE.
           05   FILLER              PIC X(3)     VALUE 'NO.'.
           05   FILLER              PIC X(6)     VALUE SPACE.
           05   FILLER              PIC X(4)     VALUE 'DATE'.
           05   FILLER              PIC X(4)     VALUE SPACE.
           05   FILLER              PIC X(6)     VALUE 'AMOUNT'.
           05   FILLER              PIC X(100)   VALUE SPACE.
      *
       01  NEXT-REPORT-LINE.
      *
           05   NRL-CC                      PIC X.
           05   NRL-ITEM-NUMBER             PIC X(5).
           05   FILLER                      PIC X(3)     VALUE SPACE.
           05   NRL-VENDOR-NUMBER           PIC Z(5).
           05   FILLER                      PIC X(3)     VALUE SPACE.
           05   NRL-RECEIPT-DATE            PIC 99B99B99.
           05   FILLER                      PIC X(3)     VALUE SPACE.
           05   NRL-RECEIPT-QUANTITY        PIC ZZZZ9.
           05   FILLER                      PIC X(100)   VALUE SPACE.
      *
       01  TOTAL-LINE-1.
      *
           05   TL1-CC                      PIC X.
           05   TL1-TRANS-PROCESSED         PIC ZZ,ZZ9.
           05   FILLER                      PIC X(23)
                                            VALUE ' TRANSACTIONS PROCESSED'.
           05   FILLER                      PIC X(103)   VALUE SPACE.
      *
       01  TOTAL-LINE-2.
      *
           05   TL2-CC                      PIC X.
           05   TL2-UNMATCHED-TRANS         PIC ZZ,ZZ9.
           05   FILLER                      PIC X(23)
                                            VALUE ' UNMATCHED TRANSACTIONS'.
           05   FILLER                      PIC X(103)   VALUE SPACE.
      *
```

Figure 2-13 Program listing for a sequential update program using a key-sequenced master file (part 3 of 6)

```
PROCEDURE DIVISION.
*
000-UPDATE-INVENTORY-FILE.
*
    OPEN INPUT  TRANFILE
         I-O    INVMSTR
         OUTPUT ERRFILE
                UPDLIST.
    PERFORM 100-UPDATE-INVENTORY-MASTER
        UNTIL TRAN-EOF.
    PERFORM 200-PRINT-TOTAL-LINES.
    CLOSE TRANFILE
          INVMSTR
          ERRFILE
          UPDLIST.
    DISPLAY 'VSKUPDT  I  1  NORMAL EOJ'.
    STOP RUN.
*
100-UPDATE-INVENTORY-MASTER.
*
    IF NEED-TRANSACTION
        PERFORM 110-READ-INVENTORY-TRANSACTION
        MOVE 'N' TO NEED-TRANSACTION-SW.
    IF NEED-MASTER
        PERFORM 120-READ-INVENTORY-MASTER
        MOVE 'N' TO NEED-MASTER-SW.
    IF NOT TRAN-EOF
        IF TR-ITEM-NUMBER EQUAL TO IM-ITEM-NUMBER
            PERFORM 130-CHANGE-INVENTORY-MASTER
            PERFORM 160-PRINT-UPDATE-LISTING
            MOVE 'Y' TO MASTER-UPDATED-SW
            MOVE 'Y' TO NEED-TRANSACTION-SW
        ELSE
            IF TR-ITEM-NUMBER GREATER THAN IM-ITEM-NUMBER
                IF MASTER-UPDATED
                    PERFORM 140-REWRITE-INVENTORY-MASTER
                    MOVE 'N' TO MASTER-UPDATED-SW
                    MOVE 'Y' TO NEED-MASTER-SW
                ELSE
                    MOVE 'Y' TO NEED-MASTER-SW
            ELSE
                PERFORM 150-WRITE-ERROR-RECORD
                MOVE 'Y' TO NEED-TRANSACTION-SW
    ELSE
        IF MASTER-UPDATED
            PERFORM 140-REWRITE-INVENTORY-MASTER.
*
110-READ-INVENTORY-TRANSACTION.
*
    READ TRANFILE INTO TR-RECORD
        AT END
            MOVE 'Y' TO TRAN-EOF-SW.
```

Figure 2-13 Program listing for a sequential update program using a key-sequenced master file (part 4 of 6)

```
     IF NOT TRAN-EOF
         ADD 1 TO TRANS-PROCESSED-COUNT.
*
 120-READ-INVENTORY-MASTER.
*
     READ INVMSTR.
     IF INVMSTR-ERROR-CODE NOT = 00
         IF INVMSTR-ERROR-CODE = 10
             MOVE HIGH-VALUE TO IM-ITEM-NUMBER
         ELSE
             DISPLAY 'VSKUPDT  A  2  READ ERROR ON INVMSTR.   '
                     'ITEM NUMBER ' IM-ITEM-NUMBER
                     '.  FILE STATUS '  INVMSTR-ERROR-CODE '.'
             MOVE 'Y' TO TRAN-EOF-SW.
*
 130-CHANGE-INVENTORY-MASTER.
*
     ADD TR-RECEIPT-QUANTITY TO IM-ON-HAND.
*
 140-REWRITE-INVENTORY-MASTER.
*
     REWRITE IM-RECORD.
     IF INVMSTR-ERROR-CODE NOT = 00
         DISPLAY 'VSKUPDT  A  3  REWRITE ERROR ON INVMSTR.    '
                     'ITEM NUMBER ' IM-ITEM-NUMBER
                     '.  FILE STATUS = ' INVMSTR-ERROR-CODE '.'
         MOVE 'Y' TO TRAN-EOF-SW.
*
 150-WRITE-ERROR-RECORD.
*
     WRITE ER-RECORD FROM TR-RECORD.
     ADD 1 TO UNMATCHED-TRANS-COUNT.
*
 160-PRINT-UPDATE-LISTING.
*
     IF LINE-COUNT GREATER THAN LINES-ON-PAGE
         PERFORM 170-PRINT-HEADING-LINES.
     MOVE TR-ITEM-NUMBER       TO NRL-ITEM-NUMBER.
     MOVE TR-VENDOR-NUMBER     TO NRL-VENDOR-NUMBER.
     MOVE TR-RECEIPT-DATE      TO NRL-RECEIPT-DATE.
     MOVE TR-RECEIPT-QUANTITY  TO NRL-RECEIPT-QUANTITY.
     MOVE NEXT-REPORT-LINE     TO PRINT-AREA.
     PERFORM 180-WRITE-REPORT-LINE.
     MOVE 1 TO SPACE-CONTROL.
*
 170-PRINT-HEADING-LINES.
*
     MOVE HDG-LINE-1 TO PRINT-AREA.
     PERFORM 190-WRITE-PAGE-TOP-LINE.
     MOVE HDG-LINE-2 TO PRINT-AREA.
     MOVE 1 TO SPACE-CONTROL.
```

Figure 2-13 Program listing for a sequential update program using a key-sequenced master file (part 5 of 6)

```
           PERFORM 180-WRITE-REPORT-LINE.
           MOVE 2 TO SPACE-CONTROL.
      *
       180-WRITE-REPORT-LINE.
      *
           WRITE PRINT-AREA
               AFTER ADVANCING SPACE-CONTROL LINES.
           ADD SPACE-CONTROL TO LINE-COUNT.
      *
       190-WRITE-PAGE-TOP-LINE.
      *
           WRITE PRINT-AREA
               AFTER ADVANCING PAGE-TOP.
           MOVE ZERO TO LINE-COUNT.
      *
       200-PRINT-TOTAL-LINES.
      *
           MOVE TRANS-PROCESSED-COUNT TO TL1-TRANS-PROCESSED.
           MOVE TOTAL-LINE-1 TO PRINT-AREA.
           MOVE 3 TO SPACE-CONTROL.
           PERFORM 180-WRITE-REPORT-LINE.
           MOVE UNMATCHED-TRANS-COUNT TO TL2-UNMATCHED-TRANS.
           MOVE TOTAL-LINE-2 TO PRINT-AREA.
           MOVE 1 TO SPACE-CONTROL.
           PERFORM 180-WRITE-REPORT-LINE.
```

Figure 2-13 Program listing for a sequential update program using a key-sequenced master file (part 6 of 6)

RANDOM PROCESSING

Figure 2-14 summarizes the COBOL elements for processing key-sequenced files randomly. These are the elements you use when updating a key-sequenced file on a random basis.

The Environment Division

The SELECT statement For random processing of a key-sequenced file, you must specify INDEXED organization and RANDOM access in the SELECT statement. You must also specify which field in the record is the RECORD KEY field. Again, the NOMINAL KEY clause is not used with VSAM files. Instead, the RECORD KEY field is used by the Procedure Division statements to locate the records they're supposed to operate on.

The Data Division

Coding in the Data Division for random processing is exactly the same as for sequential processing. The LABEL RECORDS clause is

```
IDENTIFICATION DIVISION.
    .
    .
ENVIRONMENT DIVISION.
    .
    .
INPUT-OUTPUT SECTION.
FILE-CONTROL.
    SELECT file-name ASSIGN TO assignment-name
                     ORGANIZATION IS INDEXED
                     ACCESS MODE IS RANDOM
                     RECORD KEY IS data-name
                     FILE STATUS IS data-name.
    .
    .
DATA DIVISION.
FILE SECTION.
FD  file-name
    LABEL RECORDS ARE STANDARD
    RECORD CONTAINS integer CHARACTERS.
```

Notes: 1. The RECORD KEY field must be described in the File Section as a field within the disk record.
2. The RECORDING MODE clause is invalid for VSAM.
3. The BLOCK CONTAINS clause is optional for VSAM and should not be coded.

```
    .
    .
PROCEDURE DIVISION.
    .
    .
         {INPUT   file-name ...}
    OPEN {OUTPUT  file-name ...}   ...
         {I-O     file-name ...}

    READ file-name RECORD
        [INTO data-name]
        [INVALID KEY imperative-statement].

    WRITE record-name
        [FROM data-name]
        [INVALID KEY imperative-statement].

    REWRITE record-name
        [FROM data-name]
        [INVALID KEY imperative-statement].

    DELETE file-name
        [INVALID KEY imperative-statement].

    CLOSE file-name ...
```

Figure 2-14 COBOL elements for processing key-sequenced files randomly

treated as documentation, the RECORDING MODE clause is invalid, the BLOCK CONTAINS clause should be omitted, and the RECORD KEY field must be defined in the record under the FD statement.

The Procedure Division

The READ, WRITE, REWRITE, and DELETE statements for random processing all depend on the value in the RECORD KEY field. Before a READ statement is executed, for example, the key of the desired record must be placed in the RECORD KEY field. Then, the READ statement attempts to read the record with the same key. If no such record exists, the INVALID KEY clause is executed. Likewise, the DELETE statement knows which record to delete by the value in the RECORD KEY field. And the WRITE and REWRITE statements use the RECORD KEY values to write records on output and I-O files.

When any I/O error occurs, the FILE STATUS field is updated by the system. The statements in the INVALID KEY clause are executed only for these three error conditions: record not found, duplicate key, and not enough space. Again, it's an optional clause, and since it doesn't provide for all error conditions, I recommend you omit it and instead test the FILE STATUS field with IF statements following each I/O statement.

Program example: a random update program

Figure 2-15 is a skeleton of a program that updates a key-sequenced file of inventory records on a random basis. The program has the same structure chart as the sequential update program in figure 2-12. In fact, this program is almost identical to the sequential update program. That's why I've only given a skeleton of the coding here. Any code not included is the same as figure 2-13.

For this program, I've assumed that the transaction file is in no particular sequence, so the program reads a transaction, reads the master record with the same key, changes the master record, and rewrites it. For a transaction file in sequence, however, the program should check to make sure that the updated record is rewritten back onto the disk only after all of its transactions have been processed.

In the Input-Output Section, the only change from figure 2-13 is that the SELECT statement specifies RANDOM, not SEQUENTIAL, access. As for the Procedure Division, it should be easy enough to follow. The main processing module, module 100, first reads a transaction record, moves the item number to the RECORD KEY field, and sets MASTER-FOUND-SW to Y. Then, the master file is read in module 120. If an error is detected when the master file is read, it probably indicates that no master record exists for the item number given in the RECORD KEY field (error code 23). So N is moved to MASTER-FOUND-SW, and the transaction is written on the error file. If the error code is not 23, the program is terminated. If the master is found, it is changed and rewritten, and the transaction is recorded on the update listing.

```
       IDENTIFICATION DIVISION.
      *
       PROGRAM-ID.  VSKRUPD.
      *
       ENVIRONMENT DIVISION.
      *
       INPUT-OUTPUT SECTION.
      *
       FILE-CONTROL.
           .
           .
           SELECT INVMSTR ASSIGN TO INVMSTR
                          ORGANIZATION IS INDEXED
                          ACCESS IS RANDOM
                          RECORD KEY IS IM-ITEM-NUMBER
                          FILE STATUS IS INVMSTR-ERROR-CODE.
           .
           .
      *
       DATA DIVISION.
      *
       FILE SECTION.
      *
           .
           .
       FD  INVMSTR
           LABEL RECORDS ARE STANDARD
           RECORD CONTAINS 32 CHARACTERS.
      *
       01  IM-RECORD.
      *
           05  IM-ITEM-NUMBER              PIC X(5).
           .
           .
      *
       WORKING-STORAGE SECTION.
      *
       01  SWITCHES.
      *
           05  TRAN-EOF-SW                PIC X        VALUE 'N'.
               88  TRAN-EOF                            VALUE 'Y'.
           05  MASTER-FOUND-SW            PIC X        VALUE 'N'.
               88  MASTER-FOUND                        VALUE 'Y'.
      *
           .
           .
      *
       01  FILE-STATUS-FIELD.
      *
           05  INVMSTR-ERROR-CODE         PIC XX.
      *
           .
           .
```

Figure 2-15 Partial coding for the random update program using a key-sequenced master file (part 1 of 3)

```
 PROCEDURE DIVISION.
*
 000-UPDATE-INVENTORY-FILE.
*
     OPEN INPUT  ...
          I-O     INVMSTR
          OUTPUT ...
     PERFORM 100-UPDATE-INVENTORY-MASTER
         UNTIL TRAN-EOF.
     .
     .
     CLOSE INVMSTR ...
     .
     .
*
 100-UPDATE-INVENTORY-MASTER.
*
     PERFORM 110-READ-INVENTORY-TRAN.
     IF NOT TRAN-EOF
         MOVE TR-ITEM-NUMBER TO IM-ITEM-NUMBER
         MOVE 'Y' TO MASTER-FOUND-SW
         PERFORM 120-READ-INVENTORY-MASTER
         IF MASTER-FOUND
             PERFORM 130-CHANGE-INVENTORY-MASTER
             PERFORM 140-REWRITE-INVENTORY-MASTER
             PERFORM 160-PRINT-UPDATE-LISTING
         ELSE
             PERFORM 150-WRITE-ERROR-RECORD.
*
     .
     .
*
 120-READ-INVENTORY-MASTER.
*
     READ INVMSTR.
     IF INVMSTR-ERROR-CODE NOT = 00
         IF INVMSTR-ERROR-CODE = 23
             MOVE 'N' TO MASTER-FOUND-SW
         ELSE
             DISPLAY 'VSKRUPD  A  3  READ ERROR FOR INVMSTR.  '
                     'ITEM NUMBER ' IM-ITEM-NUMBER
                     '.  FILE STATUS '  INVMSTR-ERROR-CODE
                     '.  PROGRAM TERMINATED.'
             MOVE 'N' TO MASTER-FOUND-SW
             MOVE 'Y' TO TRAN-EOF-SW.
*
 130-CHANGE-INVENTORY-MASTER.
*
     ADD TR-RECEIPT-QUANTITY TO IM-ON-HAND.
*
```

Figure 2-15 Partial coding for the random update program using a key-sequenced master file (part 2 of 3)

```
    140-REWRITE-INVENTORY-MASTER.
   *
        REWRITE IM-RECORD.
        IF INVMSTR-ERROR-CODE NOT = 00
            DISPLAY 'VSKRUPD  A  4  REWRITE ERROR FOR INVMSTR.   '
                    'ITEM NUMBER '  IM-ITEM-NUMBER
                    '.  FILE STATUS '  INVMSTR-ERROR-CODE
                    '.  PROGRAM TERMINATED.'
            MOVE 'Y' TO TRAN-EOF-SW.
```

Figure 2-15 Partial coding for the random update program using a key-sequenced master file (part 3 of 3)

Program example: a file maintenance program

File maintenance refers to the process of changing the fields within the records of a file, adding records to a file, and deleting records from a file. For example, figure 2-16 is a structure chart for an indexed file-maintenance program that provides for all three maintenance functions. Here, module 120 is the control module that determines which of four modules should be performed based on a code in the input record. Three of these modules—140, 150, and 160—actually do the work of maintaining the file. The fourth, module 170, controls the creation of the error file.

Figure 2-17 is a skeleton of the coding for the file-maintenance program. In module 120, the value of TR-ACTION-CODE is tested to determine which update action should be done. The code has three acceptable values: 'C' means a change, 'A' means an addition, and 'D' means a deletion. For changes and additions, the coding in the program is the same as it would be if the file were an ISAM file (except for the error handling statements). What I want you to see here is how deletions are handled for a VSAM key-sequenced file.

Module 160 performs the deletion function. It begins by moving the transaction item number to the RECORD KEY. Then, the DELETE statement uses the RECORD KEY value to locate and delete the inventory record. If there's not an inventory record with a matching key, the FILE STATUS field will be set to 23. The IF statement following the DELETE statement tests the FILE STATUS field. If it is zero, processing continues. Otherwise, N is moved to VALID-TRAN-SW and an appropriate error message is displayed.

When the DELETE statement is excuted for a VSAM file, the record is actually removed from the file. The space it occupied is immediately made available for file additions. Under ISAM, deleted records are indicated by the presence of a delete code (usually HIGH-VALUE in the first byte of the record). As a result, to delete records under ISAM, you must read the record, move HIGH VALUE to the delete code, and use a REWRITE statement to return the "deleted"

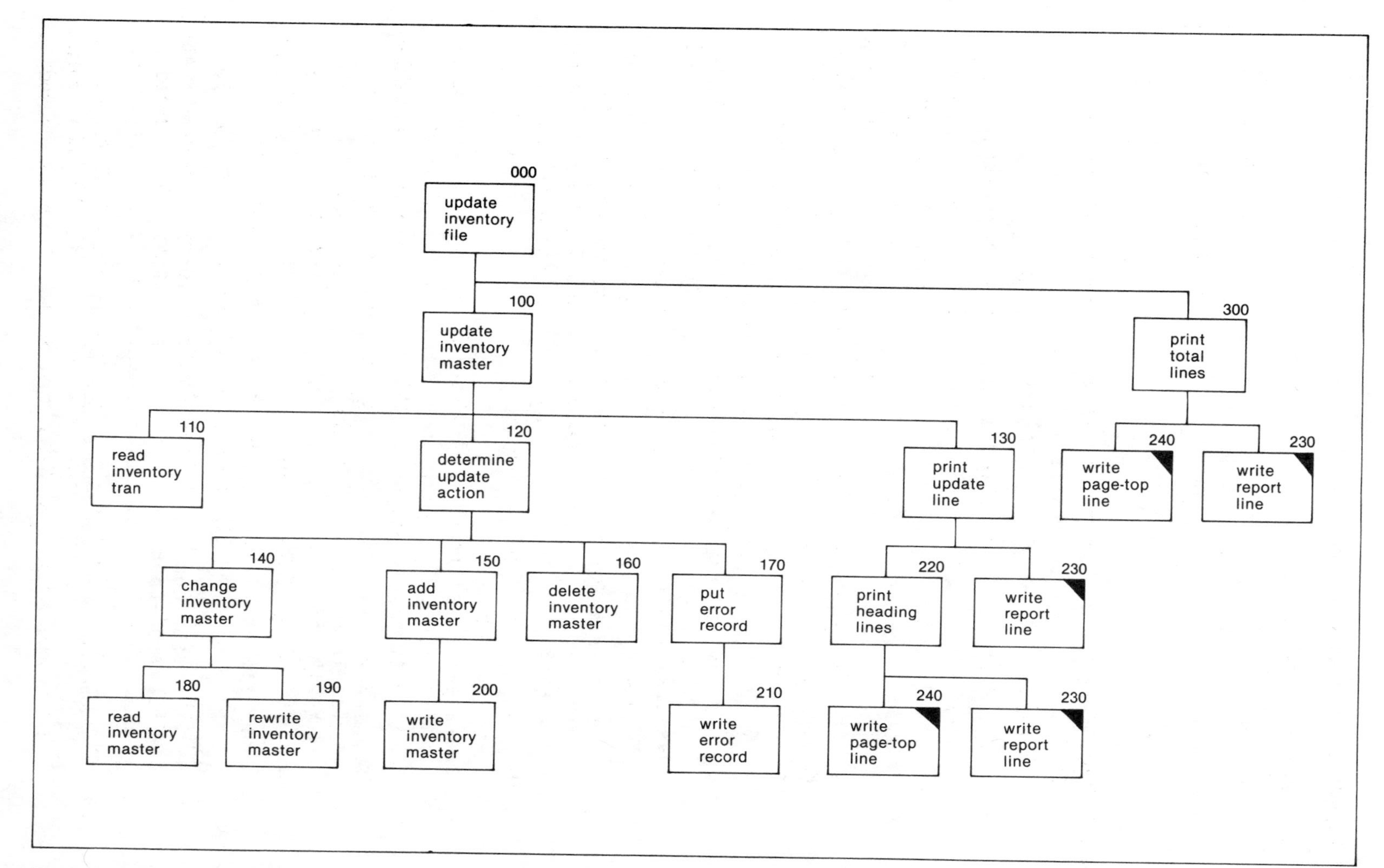

Figure 2-16 Structure chart for a file-maintenance program

```
 IDENTIFICATION DIVISION.
*
 PROGRAM-ID.  VSKMAINT.
*
 ENVIRONMENT DIVISION.
*
 INPUT-OUTPUT SECTION.
*
 FILE-CONTROL.
     .
     .
     SELECT INVMSTR ASSIGN TO INVMSTR
                    ORGANIZATION IS INDEXED
                    ACCESS IS RANDOM
                    RECORD KEY IS IM-ITEM-NUMBER
                    FILE STATUS IS INVMSTR-ERROR-CODE.
     .
     .
*
 DATA DIVISION.
*
 FILE SECTION.
*
     .
     .
 FD  INVMSTR
     LABEL RECORDS ARE STANDARD
     RECORD CONTAINS 32 CHARACTERS.
*
 01  IM-RECORD.
*
     05  IM-ITEM-NUMBER              PIC X(5).
     05  IM-ITEM-DESC                PIC X(20).
     05  IM-ON-HAND                  PIC S9(5)     COMP-3.
     05  FILLER                      PIC X(4).
*
     .
     .
 WORKING-STORAGE SECTION.
*
 01  SWITCHES.
*
     05  TRAN-EOF-SW                 PIC X         VALUE 'N'.
         88  TRAN-EOF                              VALUE 'Y'.
     05  VALID-TRAN-SW               PIC X.
         88  VALID-TRAN                            VALUE 'Y'.
*
 01  COUNT-FIELDS                    COMP-3.
*
     05  CHANGE-COUNT                PIC S9(5)     VALUE ZERO.
     05  ADDITION-COUNT              PIC S9(5)     VALUE ZERO.
     05  DELETION-COUNT              PIC S9(5)     VALUE ZERO.
```

Figure 2-17 Partial coding for the file-maintenance program using a key-sequenced master file (part 1 of 3)

```
*
 01  FILE-STATUS-FIELD.
*
     05  INVMSTR-ERROR-CODE              PIC XX.
*
 PROCEDURE DIVISION.
*
 000-UPDATE-INVENTORY-FILE.
*
     OPEN INPUT  ...
          I-O    INVMSTR
          OUTPUT ...
     PERFORM 100-UPDATE-INVENTORY-MASTER
         UNTIL TRAN-EOF.
     .
     .
     CLOSE INVMSTR ...
     .
     .
*
 100-UPDATE-INVENTORY-MASTER.
*
     PERFORM 110-READ-INVENTORY-TRAN.
     IF NOT TRAN-EOF
         PERFORM 120-DETERMINE-UPDATE-ACTION
         IF VALID-TRAN
             PERFORM 130-PRINT-UPDATE-LINE.
*
     .
     .
*
 120-DETERMINE-UPDATE-ACTION.
*
     MOVE 'Y' TO VALID-TRAN-SW.
     IF TR-ACTION-CODE = 'C'
         PERFORM 140-CHANGE-INVENTORY-MASTER
     ELSE IF TR-ACTION-CODE = 'A'
         PERFORM 150-ADD-INVENTORY-MASTER
     ELSE IF TR-ACTION-CODE = 'D'
         PERFORM 160-DELETE-INVENTORY-MASTER
     ELSE
         MOVE 'N' TO VALID-TRAN-SW.
     IF NOT VALID-TRAN
         PERFORM 170-PUT-ERROR-RECORD.
*
     .
     .
*
 150-ADD-INVENTORY-MASTER.
*
     MOVE SPACE TO IM-RECORD.
     MOVE TR-ITEM-NUMBER TO IM-ITEM-NUMBER.
```

Figure 2-17 Partial coding for the file-maintenance program using a key-sequenced master file (part 2 of 3)

```
           MOVE TR-ITEM-DESC     TO IM-ITEM-DESC.
           MOVE TR-ON-HAND       TO IM-ON-HAND.
           PERFORM 200-WRITE-INVENTORY-MASTER.
           IF VALID-TRAN
               ADD 1 TO ADDITION-COUNT.
      *
       160-DELETE-INVENTORY-MASTER.
      *
           MOVE TR-ITEM-NUMBER TO IM-ITEM-NUMBER.
           DELETE INVMSTR.
           IF INVMSTR-ERROR-CODE NOT = 00
               MOVE 'N' TO VALID-TRAN-SW
               IF INVMSTR-ERROR-CODE = 23
                   DISPLAY 'VSKMAINT  A  5  RECORD REQUESTED FOR '
                           'DELETE NOT FOUND.  ITEM NUMBER '
                           IM-ITEM-NUMBER '.'
               ELSE
                   DISPLAY 'VSKMAINT  A  6  DELETE ERROR FOR '
                           'INVMSTR.  ITEM NUMBER '
                           IM-ITEM-NUMBER '.  FILE STATUS '
                           INVMSTR-ERROR-CODE '.'.
      *
           .
           .
      *
       200-WRITE-INVENTORY-MASTER.
      *
           WRITE IM-RECORD.
           IF INVMSTR-FILE-STATUS NOT = 00
               MOVE 'N' TO VALID-TRAN-SW
               IF INVMSTR-FILE-STATUS = 22
                   DISPLAY 'VSKMAINT  A  7  RECORD REQUESTED FOR '
                           'ADDITION HAS DUPLICATE KEY.  '
                           'ITEM NUMBER ' IM-ITEM-NUMBER '.'
               ELSE
                   DISPLAY 'VSKMAINT  A  8  WRITE ERROR FOR '
                           'INVMSTR.  ITEM NUMBER '
                           IM-ITEM-NUMBER '.  FILE STATUS '
                           INVMSTR-ERROR-CODE '.'.
      *
           .
           .
```

Figure 2-17 Partial coding for the file-maintenance program using a key-sequenced master file (part 3 of 3)

record to the file. Any program that subsequently processes the file must check for these deleted records. This isn't true for VSAM—once you use the DELETE statement to remove a record from the file, you never have to worry about it again.

DISCUSSION

At this point, you should be ready to begin writing COBOL programs to process VSAM files. For your reference, here is a summary of the significant differences between VSAM and ISAM COBOL:

1. The VSAM SELECT statement is different in these respects:
   a. The assignment name doesn't require the class or device type fields, just the file's ddname.
   b. The ORGANIZATION IS INDEXED clause is required.
   c. The FILE STATUS clause should always be used.
   d. The NOMINAL KEY clause isn't used for VSAM; instead, the RECORD KEY clause is used.
2. In the Data Division, the FD statement has two variations:
   a. The RECORDING MODE clause is invalid for VSAM.
   b. The BLOCK CONTAINS clause is optional and should be omitted for VSAM.
3. The START statement for VSAM files is extended to allow the KEY option.
4. The INVALID KEY clause is optional on all I/O statements, and isn't recommended. Instead, code IF statements to test the FILE STATUS values after every I/O statement.
5. The DELETE statement is implemented for VSAM. As a result, it isn't necessary to test for dummy records in a VSAM file.

In the next topic, I will discuss VSAM error handling in more detail. Why? Because there are some additional error handling problems that you should know about and provide for in your COBOL programs. So be sure to read topic 3. I've deliberately simplified the presentation of error handling in this topic.

Terminology

file maintenance

Objectives

1. Given a problem involving VSAM key-sequenced files, code a COBOL solution.

Problems

1. Assume an ISAM inventory-master file was converted to VSAM three months before the inventory-file maintenance program was modified to process it as a VSAM file. In the meantime, the

ISAM version of the maintenance program was used to process the VSAM file using the ISAM interface. Now, because of the way the ISAM program handled deletions, the VSAM file contains several hundred inactive records, indicated by a delete code (HIGH-VALUE in the first byte of each deleted record). Write a COBOL program to reorganize the file by deleting all the records marked as inactive. The format of the inventory record is this:

Field name	Delete code	Item no.	Item description	On hand	Unused
Characteristics	X	X(5)	X(20)	S9(5)	X(3)
Usage				COMP-3	
Position	1	2-6	7-26	27-29	30-32

Each time a record is deleted, display a message showing the record's item number. The ddname for the VSAM file should be INVMSTR.

Solutions

1. Figure 2-18 shows an acceptable structure chart for this program. Figure 2-19 shows a COBOL program based on this structure chart. As the file is processed sequentially, each record is checked to see if it has been marked for deletion. If so, the record is deleted by the DELETE statement in module 120 and a message is displayed.

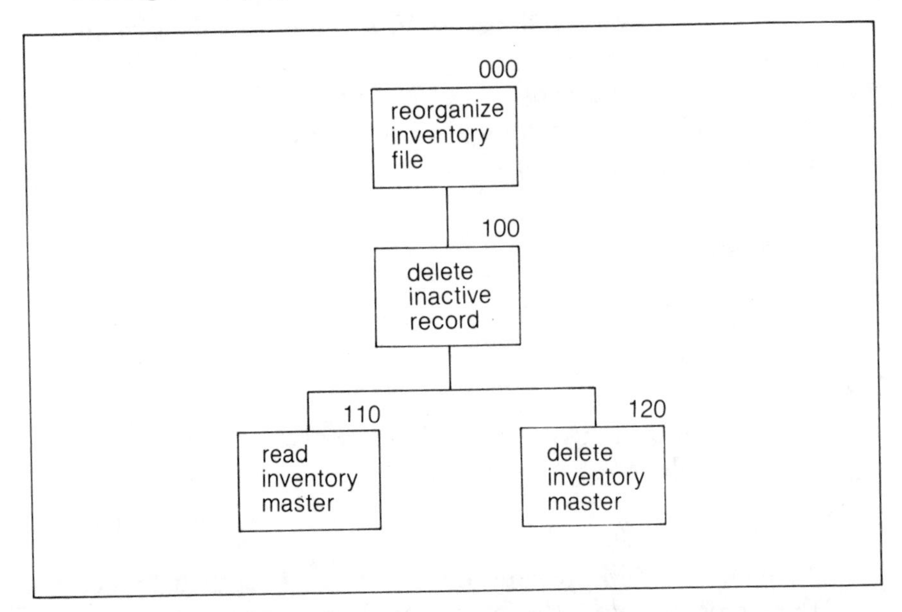

Figure 2-18 Structure chart for the indexed file-reorganization program

```
 IDENTIFICATION DIVISION.
*
 PROGRAM-ID.  VSKREORG.
*
 ENVIRONMENT DIVISION.
*
 INPUT-OUTPUT SECTION.
*
 FILE-CONTROL.
     SELECT INVMSTR   ASSIGN TO INVMSTR
                      ORGANIZATION IS INDEXED
                      ACCESS IS SEQUENTIAL
                      RECORD KEY IS IM-ITEM-NUMBER
                      FILE STATUS IS INVMSTR-ERROR-CODE.
*
 DATA DIVISION.
*
 FILE SECTION.
*
 FD  INVMSTR
     LABEL RECORDS ARE STANDARD
     RECORD CONTAINS 32 CHARACTERS.
*
 01  IM-RECORD.
*
     05  IM-DELETE-CODE   PIC X.
     05  IM-ITEM-NUMBER   PIC X(5).
     05  IM-ITEM-DESC     PIC X(20).
     05  IM-ON-HAND       PIC S9(5)   COMP-3.
     05  FILLER           PIC X(3).
*
 WORKING-STORAGE SECTION.
*
 01  SWITCHES.
*
     05  INVMSTR-EOF-SW       PIC X   VALUE 'N'.
         88  INVMSTR-EOF              VALUE 'Y'.
*
 01  FILE-STATUS-FIELD.
*
     05  INVMSTR-ERROR-CODE  PIC XX.
*
 PROCEDURE DIVISION.
*
 000-REORGANIZE-INVENTORY-FILE.
*
     OPEN I-O INVMSTR.
     PERFORM 100-DELETE-INACTIVE-RECORD
         UNTIL INVMSTR-EOF.
     CLOSE INVMSTR.
     DISPLAY 'VSKREORG  I  1  NORMAL EOJ'.
     STOP RUN.
```

Figure 2-19 Program listing for the indexed file-reorganization program (part 1 of 2)

```
*
 100-DELETE-INACTIVE-RECORD.
*
     PERFORM 110-READ-INVENTORY-MASTER.
     IF NOT INVMSTR-EOF
         IF IM-DELETE-CODE EQUAL HIGH-VALUE
             PERFORM 120-DELETE-INVENTORY-MASTER
             DISPLAY 'VSKREORG  I  2  RECORD DELETED.  '
                     'ITEM NUMBER '  IM-ITEM-NUMBER.
*
 110-READ-INVENTORY-MASTER.
*
     READ INVMSTR.
     IF INVMSTR-ERROR-CODE NOT = 00
         IF INVMSTR-ERROR-CODE = 10
             MOVE 'Y' TO INVMSTR-EOF-SW
         ELSE
             DISPLAY 'VSKREORG  A  3  READ ERROR ON INVMSTR.  '
                     'ITEM NUMBER '  IM-ITEM-NUMBER
                     '.  FILE STATUS '  INVMSTR-ERROR-CODE '.'
             MOVE 'Y' TO INVMSTR-EOF-SW.
*
 120-DELETE-INVENTORY-MASTER.
*
     DELETE INVMSTR.
     IF INVMSTR-ERROR-CODE NOT = 00
         DISPLAY 'VSKREORG  A  4  DELETE ERROR ON INVMSTR.  '
                 'ITEM NUMBER '  IM-ITEM-NUMBER.
```

Figure 2-19 Program listing for the indexed file-reorganization program (part 2 of 2)

TOPIC 3 VSAM Error Processing

Because of the way VSAM handles error conditions, many I/O errors that caused programs to abend under ISAM do not cause an abend for VSAM. Instead, the FILE STATUS field is set to indicate the nature of the problem, a message is printed in the JCL listing, and control returns to the COBOL program. As a result, the program is responsible for testing the FILE STATUS field and taking the necessary action if an error has occurred. If the program doesn't test the FILE STATUS field, serious errors could go undetected.

To illustrate, suppose a key-sequenced master file is updated on a sequential basis. When the cluster was defined (perhaps several years ago), it was given enough space to hold 10,000 records—more than enough for its expected 2,000 records. As the company grew, so did its master file. Now it contains 9,800 records. No one ever noticed that it was approaching its space limit. In this update run, 400 new records are added to the file—thus exceeding the file's space allocation by 200 records. Normally, you would expect the system to terminate the program when it attempts to write a record beyond the space allocated to the file, with a return code indicating that the file's space has been exhausted (probably D37). Under VSAM, however, the operating system doesn't take over. Instead, VSAM prints a warning message in the JCL listing, sets the FILE STATUS field to 24, and returns control to the statement following the WRITE statement. If the COBOL program doesn't test the FILE STATUS field, it will assume that the record has been successfully written to the file when actually the record is lost. So, the program reads another transaction, tries to write it to the master file, assumes it has been successfully written, and continues. That record is lost too. In fact, all 200 of the records that are written after the file's limit of 10,000 records is reached are lost.

Granted, the operating system does print a message indicating that an error has occurred. In fact, it prints a message for each unsuccessful I/O operation. So the JCL listing for this program would contain 200 messages indicating that the program didn't work. But how can you guarantee that those messages will be noticed? It's likely in fact that the only thing the operator will notice is that the update program terminated normally. But that just means the program didn't abend—it doesn't mean there were no errors. Typically, an error of this nature goes undetected for several days—perhaps even a week. I know of one installation that completely lost a master file and didn't discover it for five days—after its generation backup cycle had completed and the only remaining backup of the master file was a volume backup a month old. I'm sure you can appreciate the difficulties this installation faced trying to explain its problem to management.

COBOL processing for VSAM errors

As I have already mentioned, the only way to avoid the problems caused by undetected error conditions is to test the FILE STATUS field after every I/O statement to ensure that no error has occurred. If there is no error, processing may continue. If there is a serious error, you should terminate the program. In the programming examples in the last topic, I did just that. After each I/O statement (except OPEN and CLOSE—I'll get to them in just a moment), I coded an IF statement to test the FILE STATUS field. To illustrate, consider these statements:

```
WRITE IM-RECORD.
IF INVMSTR-ERROR-CODE NOT = 00
    DISPLAY 'VSKCR A 1 WRITE ERROR FOR INVMSTR. '
            'FILE STATUS ' INVMSTR-ERROR-CODE
            '. PROGRAM TERMINATED.'
    MOVE 'Y' TO INVCARDS-EOF-SW.
```

In this case, if the WRITE statement tries to write a record beyond the space allocated to the file, VSAM moves a value of 24 to INVMSTR-ERROR-CODE (the FILE STATUS field). Then, the IF statement causes the message

```
VSKCR A 1 WRITE ERROR FOR INVMSTR. FILE
STATUS 24. PROGRAM TERMINATED.
```

to be displayed in the job output (on one line, of course). The program is terminated by moving Y to the end-of-file switch.

In addition to READ, WRITE, REWRITE, START, and DELETE statements, error checking should be done after OPEN and CLOSE statements. It isn't absolutely necessary to test for errors after an OPEN statement, because even if an open error is ignored, the first READ or WRITE statement for the file will fail because the file was not properly opened. However, I recommend that you test the FILE STATUS field after an OPEN statement. It's only a few lines of code, and it can save you debugging time if an open error does occur.

As for the CLOSE statement, I recommend that you check for errors after its execution too. If a close error occurs and is undetected, it won't be discovered until the next time an open is issued for the file—maybe a few hours later, maybe a few days. As a result, it could be difficult to find the program that caused the problem. (For the sake of clarity, I didn't check for OPEN and CLOSE errors in the programs in the last topic.)

Although the method of error handling just described is better than none at all, it has two serious drawbacks. First, if the error messages printed by the system are ignored, why would anyone notice the error messages printed by the COBOL program? Second, if the program is part of a procedure involving several job steps, the steps following the program will still be executed—even though the program failed. (Remember that even though you set a switch to terminate your program, the program still ends normally as far as OS is concerned.)

The solution to both these problems is to provide a means for your COBOL program to terminate abnormally. Since operators are trained to look for jobs that terminate abnormally, it isn't likely that they'll miss it. And when a job step is abnormally terminated, the steps that follow aren't executed.

Unfortunately, COBOL provides no direct means for abnormal program termination. But it is easy to write an assembler-language subprogram that can be called whenever you wish to terminate your program abnormally. Figure 2-20 illustrates two OS assembler subprograms that can be used for this purpose. (DOS versions of these subprograms are shown in chapter 6.) The first subprogram in figure 2-20, called ABEND100, terminates the program abnormally, setting the user return code to 100. The second subprogram, ABEND200,

Abend without dump

```
ABEND100   START   0
           SAVE    (14,12)
           ABEND   100
           END
```

Abend with dump

```
ABEND200   START   0
           SAVE    (14,12)
           ABEND   200,DUMP
           END
```

Figure 2-20 OS assembler language subprograms for terminating a COBOL program

operates the same except that a storage dump is printed and the user return code is 200. When ABEND200 is used, you must include a SYSUDUMP or SYSABEND DD statement in your JCL or the dump won't print. Many installations already have subprograms similar to these. If yours doesn't, feel free to use the ones in figure 2-20.

Figure 2-21 shows a VSAM program that uses the ABEND200 subprogram to terminate the program in the event of an error condition. This is the sequential-update program originally presented in figures 2-12 and 2-13. Now, however, the program does a more complete job of error handling by checking the FILE STATUS field after all I/O statements (OPEN, CLOSE, and REWRITE). If a serious error is detected, the program uses a common module—module 300—to invoke the abend subprogram. Module 300 first displays a message showing the FILE STATUS value and indicating that the program is being terminated. Then, this statement

```
CALL 'ABEND200'.
```

is used to invoke the assembler language subprogram. When this CALL statement is executed, a storage dump is printed and the job is terminated. Control never returns to the COBOL program.

Unfortunately, this practice violates one of the basic rules of structured programming—that every called module must return to the module that called it. Although it is possible to set up code that adheres to this rule, I think it would be foolish. It would involve major changes in nearly all of the modules of the program. Since unrecoverable error conditions are rare, I think it is best to call the abend subprogram from wherever the error occurs and not worry about returning to the calling module.

```
 IDENTIFICATION DIVISION.
*
 PROGRAM-ID.  VSKSUPDT.
*
 ENVIRONMENT DIVISION.
*
 CONFIGURATION SECTION.
*
 SPECIAL-NAMES.
     C01 IS PAGE-TOP.
*
 INPUT-OUTPUT SECTION.
*
 FILE-CONTROL.
     SELECT TRANFILE ASSIGN TO UT-S-TRANFILE.
     SELECT INVMSTR  ASSIGN TO INVMSTR
                     ORGANIZATION IS INDEXED
                     ACCESS IS SEQUENTIAL
                     RECORD KEY IS IM-ITEM-NUMBER
                     FILE STATUS IS INVMSTR-ERROR-CODE.
     SELECT ERRFILE  ASSIGN TO UT-S-ERRFILE.
     SELECT UPDLIST  ASSIGN TO UT-S-UPDLIST.
*
 DATA DIVISION.
*
 FILE SECTION.
*
 FD  TRANFILE
     LABEL RECORDS ARE STANDARD
     RECORDING MODE IS F
     RECORD CONTAINS 24 CHARACTERS
     BLOCK CONTAINS 0 RECORDS.
*
 01  TR-AREA                 PIC X(24).
*
 FD  INVMSTR
     LABEL RECORDS ARE STANDARD
     RECORD CONTAINS 32 CHARACTERS.
*
 01  IM-RECORD.
*
     05  IM-ITEM-NUMBER      PIC X(5).
     05  IM-ITEM-DESC        PIC X(20).
     05  IM-ON-HAND          PIC S9(5)       COMP-3.
     05  FILLER              PIC X(4).
*
 FD  ERRFILE
     LABEL RECORDS ARE STANDARD
     RECORDING MODE IS F
     RECORD CONTAINS 24 CHARACTERS
     BLOCK CONTAINS 0 RECORDS.
*
```

Figure 2-21 Program listing for a sequential update program that handles all I/O error conditions and uses abnormal program termination when appropriate (part 1 of 6)

```
 01   ER-RECORD              PIC X(24).
*
 FD   UPDLIST
      LABEL RECORDS ARE OMITTED
      RECORDING MODE IS F
      RECORD CONTAINS 133 CHARACTERS
      BLOCK CONTAINS 0 RECORDS.
*
 01   PRINT-AREA             PIC X(133).
*
 WORKING-STORAGE SECTION.
*
 01   SWITCHES.
*
      05   TRAN-EOF-SW                     PIC X     VALUE 'N'.
           88   TRAN-EOF                             VALUE 'Y'.
      05   NEED-TRANSACTION-SW             PIC X     VALUE 'Y'.
           88   NEED-TRANSACTION                     VALUE 'Y'.
      05   NEED-MASTER-SW                  PIC X     VALUE 'Y'.
           88   NEED-MASTER                          VALUE 'Y'.
      05   MASTER-UPDATED-SW               PIC X     VALUE 'N'.
           88   MASTER-UPDATED                       VALUE 'Y'.
*
 01   FILE-STATUS-FIELD.
*
      05   INVMSTR-ERROR-CODE        PIC XX.
*
 01   COUNT-FIELDS                   COMP-3.
*
      05   TRANS-PROCESSED-COUNT     PIC S9(5)       VALUE ZERO.
      05   UNMATCHED-TRANS-COUNT     PIC S9(5)       VALUE ZERO.
*
 01   PRINT-FIELDS                   COMP            SYNC.
*
      05   LINE-COUNT                PIC S99         VALUE +99.
      05   LINES-ON-PAGE             PIC S99         VALUE +57.
      05   SPACE-CONTROL             PIC S9.
*
 01   TR-RECORD.
*
      05   TR-ITEM-NUMBER            PIC X(5).
      05   TR-VENDOR-NUMBER          PIC X(5).
      05   TR-RECEIPT-DATE           PIC X(6).
      05   TR-RECEIPT-QUANTITY       PIC S9(5)       COMP-3.
      05   FILLER                    PIC X(5).
*
 01   HDG-LINE-1.
*
      05   HDG1-CC             PIC X.
      05   FILLER              PIC X(1)     VALUE SPACE.
      05   FILLER              PIC X(4)     VALUE 'ITEM'.
      05   FILLER              PIC X(2)     VALUE SPACE.
```

Figure 2-21 Program listing for a sequential update program that handles all I/O error conditions and uses abnormal program termination when appropriate (part 2 of 6)

```
           05  FILLER            PIC X(6)     VALUE 'VENDOR'.
           05  FILLER            PIC X(4)     VALUE SPACE.
           05  FILLER            PIC X(7)     VALUE 'RECEIPT'.
           05  FILLER            PIC X(2)     VALUE SPACE.
           05  FILLER            PIC X(7)     VALUE 'RECEIPT'.
           05  FILLER            PIC X(99)    VALUE SPACE.
      *
       01  HDG-LINE-2.
      *
           05  HDG2-CC           PIC X.
           05  FILLER            PIC X(2)     VALUE SPACE.
           05  FILLER            PIC X(3)     VALUE 'NO.'.
           05  FILLER            PIC X(4)     VALUE SPACE.
           05  FILLER            PIC X(3)     VALUE 'NO.'.
           05  FILLER            PIC X(6)     VALUE SPACE.
           05  FILLER            PIC X(4)     VALUE 'DATE'.
           05  FILLER            PIC X(4)     VALUE SPACE.
           05  FILLER            PIC X(6)     VALUE 'AMOUNT'.
           05  FILLER            PIC X(100)   VALUE SPACE.
      *
       01  NEXT-REPORT-LINE.
      *
           05  NRL-CC                     PIC X.
           05  NRL-ITEM-NUMBER            PIC X(5).
           05  FILLER                     PIC X(3)     VALUE SPACE.
           05  NRL-VENDOR-NUMBER          PIC Z(5).
           05  FILLER                     PIC X(3)     VALUE SPACE.
           05  NRL-RECEIPT-DATE           PIC 99B99B99.
           05  FILLER                     PIC X(3)     VALUE SPACE.
           05  NRL-RECEIPT-QUANTITY       PIC ZZZZ9.
           05  FILLER                     PIC X(100)   VALUE SPACE.
      *
       01  TOTAL-LINE-1.
      *
           05  TL1-CC                     PIC X.
           05  TL1-TRANS-PROCESSED        PIC ZZ,ZZ9.
           05  FILLER                     PIC X(23)
                                          VALUE ' TRANSACTIONS PROCESSED'.
           05  FILLER                     PIC X(103)   VALUE SPACE.
      *
       01  TOTAL-LINE-2.
      *
           05  TL2-CC                     PIC X.
           05  TL2-UNMATCHED-TRANS        PIC ZZ,ZZ9.
           05  FILLER                     PIC X(23)
                                          VALUE ' UNMATCHED TRANSACTIONS'.
           05  FILLER                     PIC X(103)   VALUE SPACE.
      *
       PROCEDURE DIVISION.
      *
       000-UPDATE-INVENTORY-FILE.
      *
```

Figure 2-21 Program listing for a sequential update program that handles all I/O error conditions and uses abnormal program termination when appropriate (part 3 of 6)

```
           OPEN INPUT  TRANFILE
                I-O    INVMSTR
                OUTPUT ERRFILE
                       UPDLIST.
           IF INVMSTR-ERROR-CODE NOT = 00
               DISPLAY 'VSKSUPDT  A  2  OPEN ERROR ON INVMSTR.'
               PERFORM 300-TERMINATE-UPDATE-PROGRAM.
           PERFORM 100-UPDATE-INVENTORY-MASTER
               UNTIL TRAN-EOF.
           PERFORM 200-PRINT-TOTAL-LINES.
           CLOSE TRANFILE
                 INVMSTR
                 ERRFILE
                 UPDLIST.
           IF INVMSTR-ERROR-CODE NOT = 00
               DISPLAY 'VSKSUPDT  A  3  CLOSE ERROR ON INVMSTR.'
               PERFORM 300-TERMINATE-UPDATE-PROGRAM.
           DISPLAY 'VSKUPDT  I  1  NORMAL EOJ'.
           STOP RUN.
      *
       100-UPDATE-INVENTORY-MASTER.
      *
           IF NEED-TRANSACTION
               PERFORM 110-READ-INVENTORY-TRANSACTION
               MOVE 'N' TO NEED-TRANSACTION-SW.
           IF NEED-MASTER
               PERFORM 120-READ-INVENTORY-MASTER
               MOVE 'N' TO NEED-MASTER-SW.
           IF NOT TRAN-EOF
               IF TR-ITEM-NUMBER EQUAL TO IM-ITEM-NUMBER
                   PERFORM 130-CHANGE-INVENTORY-MASTER
                   PERFORM 160-PRINT-UPDATE-LISTING
                   MOVE 'Y' TO MASTER-UPDATED-SW
                   MOVE 'Y' TO NEED-TRANSACTION-SW
               ELSE
                   IF TR-ITEM-NUMBER GREATER THAN IM-ITEM-NUMBER
                       IF MASTER-UPDATED
                           PERFORM 140-REWRITE-INVENTORY-MASTER
                           MOVE 'N' TO MASTER-UPDATED-SW
                           MOVE 'Y' TO NEED-MASTER-SW
                       ELSE
                           MOVE 'Y' TO NEED-MASTER-SW
                   ELSE
                       PERFORM 150-WRITE-ERROR-RECORD
                       MOVE 'Y' TO NEED-TRANSACTION-SW
           ELSE
               IF MASTER-UPDATED
                   PERFORM 140-REWRITE-INVENTORY-MASTER.
      *
       110-READ-INVENTORY-TRANSACTION.
      *
```

Figure 2-21 Program listing for a sequential update program that handles all I/O error conditions and uses abnormal program termination when appropriate (part 4 of 6)

```
           READ TRANFILE INTO TR-RECORD
               AT END
                   MOVE 'Y' TO TRAN-EOF-SW.
           IF NOT TRAN-EOF
               ADD 1 TO TRANS-PROCESSED-COUNT.
      *
       120-READ-INVENTORY-MASTER.
      *
           READ INVMSTR.
           IF INVMSTR-ERROR-CODE NOT = 00
               IF INVMSTR-ERROR-CODE = 10
                   MOVE HIGH-VALUE TO IM-ITEM-NUMBER
               ELSE
                   DISPLAY 'VSKSUPDT  A  4  READ ERROR ON INVMSTR.   '
                           'ITEM NUMBER ' IM-ITEM-NUMBER  '.'
                   PERFORM 300-TERMINATE-UPDATE-PROGRAM.
      *
       130-CHANGE-INVENTORY-MASTER.
      *
           ADD TR-RECEIPT-QUANTITY TO IM-ON-HAND.
      *
       140-REWRITE-INVENTORY-MASTER.
      *
           REWRITE IM-RECORD.
           IF INVMSTR-ERROR-CODE NOT = 00
               DISPLAY 'VSKSUPDT  A  5  REWRITE ERROR ON INVMSTR.   '
                       'ITEM NUMBER ' IM-ITEM-NUMBER  '.'
               PERFORM 300-TERMINATE-UPDATE-PROGRAM.
      *
       150-WRITE-ERROR-RECORD.
      *
           WRITE ER-RECORD FROM TR-RECORD.
           ADD 1 TO UNMATCHED-TRANS-COUNT.
      *
       160-PRINT-UPDATE-LISTING.
      *
           IF LINE-COUNT GREATER THAN LINES-ON-PAGE
               PERFORM 170-PRINT-HEADING-LINES.
           MOVE TR-ITEM-NUMBER      TO NRL-ITEM-NUMBER.
           MOVE TR-VENDOR-NUMBER    TO NRL-VENDOR-NUMBER.
           MOVE TR-RECEIPT-DATE     TO NRL-RECEIPT-DATE.
           MOVE TR-RECEIPT-QUANTITY TO NRL-RECEIPT-QUANTITY.
           MOVE NEXT-REPORT-LINE    TO PRINT-AREA.
           PERFORM 180-WRITE-REPORT-LINE.
           MOVE 1 TO SPACE-CONTROL.
      *
       170-PRINT-HEADING-LINES.
      *
           MOVE HDG-LINE-1 TO PRINT-AREA.
           PERFORM 190-WRITE-PAGE-TOP-LINE.
           MOVE HDG-LINE-2 TO PRINT-AREA.
           MOVE 1 TO SPACE-CONTROL.
```

Figure 2-21 Program listing for a sequential update program that handles all I/O error conditions and uses abnormal program termination when appropriate (part 5 of 6)

```
           PERFORM 180-WRITE-REPORT-LINE.
           MOVE 2 TO SPACE-CONTROL.
      *
       180-WRITE-REPORT-LINE.
      *
           WRITE PRINT-AREA
               AFTER ADVANCING SPACE-CONTROL LINES.
           ADD SPACE-CONTROL TO LINE-COUNT.
      *
       190-WRITE-PAGE-TOP-LINE.
      *
           WRITE PRINT-AREA
               AFTER ADVANCING PAGE-TOP.
           MOVE ZERO TO LINE-COUNT.
      *
       200-PRINT-TOTAL-LINES.
      *
           MOVE TRANS-PROCESSED-COUNT TO TL1-TRANS-PROCESSED.
           MOVE TOTAL-LINE-1 TO PRINT-AREA.
           MOVE 3 TO SPACE-CONTROL.
           PERFORM 180-WRITE-REPORT-LINE.
           MOVE UNMATCHED-TRANS-COUNT TO TL2-UNMATCHED-TRANS.
           MOVE TOTAL-LINE-2 TO PRINT-AREA.
           MOVE 1 TO SPACE-CONTROL.
           PERFORM 180-WRITE-REPORT-LINE.
      *
       300-TERMINATE-UPDATE-PROGRAM.
      *
           DISPLAY 'VSKSUPDT  A  6  ABENDING WITH DUMP VIA ABEND200.
                   'FILE STATUS '  INVMSTR-ERROR-CODE  '.'.
           CALL 'ABEND200'.
```

Figure 2-21 Program listing for a sequential update program that handles all I/O error conditions and uses abnormal program termination when appropriate (part 6 of 6)

FILE STATUS error codes

In the last topic, I showed you the FILE STATUS values that are commonly encountered with key-sequenced files. Most of these codes represent recoverable conditions: end of file, duplicate key, out-of-sequence record, and record not found. But FILE STATUS codes are also used to indicate unrecoverable errors. For example, you already know that code 24 means the file has run out of space. There is no way to recover from this error—the program must be terminated and rerun after additional space has been allocated to the file.

Figure 2-22 lists all of the possible FILE STATUS values for key-sequenced files. This table lists the meaning of the FILE STATUS

FILE STATUS value	OPEN	CLOSE	READ	WRITE	REWRITE	DELETE	START	Recommended program action
00	File successfully opened	File successfully closed	Record successfully read	Record successfully written	Record successfully rewritten	Record successfully deleted	Successful completion	Continue processing
10			End of file reached					Normal AT END processing
21				Record out of sequence (sequential access only)				Print error message and continue
22				Duplicate key				Print error message and continue
23			Record not found			Record not found	Specified key not found	For READ and DELETE: Print error message and continue For START: Use default key or terminate program
24				No more space allocated to file				Terminate job
30	Uncorrectable I/O error	Uncorrectable I/O error	Uncorrectable I/O error	Uncorrectable I/O error	Uncorrectable I/O error	Uncorrectable I/O error	Uncorrectable I/O error	Terminate job
90	Unusable file—possibly an empty file opened as I/O	VSAM logic error	VSAM logic error	VSAM logic error	VSAM logic error	VSAM logic error	VSAM logic error	Terminate job

Figure 2-22 Complete table of FILE STATUS values for key-sequenced files (part 1 of 2)

FILE STATUS value	OPEN	CLOSE	READ	WRITE	REWRITE	DELETE	START	Recommended program action
91	Password failure							Terminate job
92	File already opened	File not open	File is not open or end of file already reached	File is not open; incorrect key for EXTEND file	File is not open; no previous READ	File is not open; no previous READ (sequential access)	Invalid request; probably file not open	Terminate job
93	Not enough virtual storage for VSAM task	Not enough virtual storage for VSAM task	Not enough virtual storage for VSAM task	Not enough virtual storage for VSAM task	Not enough virtual storage for VSAM task	Not enough virtual storage for VSAM task	Not enough virtual storage for VSAM task	Terminate job
95	Conflicting file attributes							Terminate job
96	No DD statement							Terminate job
97	File not closed by previous job							Terminate job

Figure 2-22 Complete table of FILE STATUS values for key-sequenced files (part 2 of 2)

codes for each I/O statement, and gives a recommendation on how to handle the error.

All of the codes that are 24 or higher represent serious error conditions that generally can't be corrected by the COBOL program. As a result, the recommended action for these codes is program termination. Of course, specific program requirements or local standards may dictate some other action. But in most cases, I think it is best to terminate the program when one of these errors occurs.

FILE STATUS codes 30, 90, and 93 represent system errors that don't often occur, so you won't encounter these codes often. Code 30 usually indicates a hardware problem such as a parity error or transmission error. Code 90 indicates some type of VSAM logic error. It might be caused by a bug in the COBOL compiler or in the VSAM system itself. Or, this code could occur if some VSAM system data has inadvertently been destroyed. Code 93 means that you didn't allocate enough virtual storage for VSAM to perform an I/O operation. If this error occurs, simply allocate more storage and rerun the job. As I said, these error codes are not common, so you won't see them often.

If the FILE STATUS is 92, it means you tried to do something that isn't allowed. Common causes of code 92 are trying to read or write records to a file that hasn't been opened, trying to rewrite a record (using sequential access) before a record has been successfully read, or attempting to read a record after the end of file has been reached. In any event, the error is caused by a logic problem in your COBOL program, so it's best to terminate the program before it does more damage.

Some of the FILE STATUS codes (91, 95, 96, and 97) are only caused by OPEN errors. Code 91 means your COBOL program is denied access to the file because it didn't supply a proper password. If your installation uses password protection for its files, you may encounter this error from time to time. Code 95 means the file has conflicting attributes. For example, a COBOL program may have specified that the file's record key is in positions 2-9 but the file was defined with its key in positions 4-11. Code 96 means there is no DD statement for the file. Finally, code 97 means that the file hasn't been closed. Usually, this means that a previous program failed to close the file, either because of a programming error or an abnormal termination. Although it is possible to continue processing (VSAM automatically issues a CLOSE before it opens the file), it isn't advisable. If a previous program aborted while it was processing the file, it's best to wait until you find out what caused it to abort before you process the file again.

Discussion

The purpose of this topic is to convince you of the need for error processing in VSAM COBOL programs. I hope you are now convinced. If you neglect to test the FILE STATUS field after every I/O statement, major errors could go unnoticed. Such errors are difficult to track down after the fact.

However, I must point out that the methods presented here for handling VSAM error conditions are not standard throughout the industry. Local standards may require that you use some other method. One common error-processing technique is to code a detailed reporting procedure that clearly indicates the error. Such a procedure may attempt to recover from the error, although in most cases this is not really possible. Another procedure is to use the special register RETURN-CODE to pass a code back to the JCL. Then, subsequent EXEC statements in the JCL test the return code to determine if the job should continue. (This facility is not available to DOS users.) In any event, be sure that your COBOL programs process error conditions in a way that is acceptable to your installation.

If the need for detailed error processing in the COBOL program seems unfortunate to you, take heart. Many large COBOL users are upset about the problem and are urging IBM to improve the situation with the next release of the VS COBOL compiler. In the meantime, several compiler patches are available to modify the COBOL compiler so unusual error conditions will cause an abend. Of course, most installations do not have such a patch installed, so don't assume that you can get away without proper error-checking in your COBOL programs.

One question you may be asking right now is this: Is it really necessary to perform detailed error checking in *all* VSAM COBOL programs? The answer to this question is probably, no. In programs that don't actually write data to a VSAM file, you can usually get away with limited error checking. For example, consider what might happen if an uncorrectable I/O error occurs during a report-preparation program. Even if the program assumes that a record has been properly read when it really hasn't, the fact that no data has been read will undoubtedly cause the program to abend when it tries to process the data. So for simple report preparation programs and other programs that don't change the data in a VSAM file, detailed error checking isn't really necessary. But for any program that changes the data in a VSAM file, error checking is a must.

DOS users must be aware that everything I said in this topic about error handling on an OS system is true on a DOS system as well. The only difference is that there are a few minor variations in the error codes returned to the FILE STATUS field. So DOS VSAM users must provide for error processing in their COBOL programs just as OS users must.

Objectives

1. Explain why COBOL error-processing is so crucial when using VSAM.
2. Given a complete COBOL program that processes VSAM files, make modifications to the program so that it properly handles I/O error conditions.

Problems

1. Figure 2-10 is an indexed file-creation program. Make the necessary modifications to this program so that it properly handles error conditions. When an unrecoverable I/O error occurs, the program should be terminated and a storage dump should be printed.

Solutions

1. Figure 2-23 is an acceptable solution. A common module has been added to call the ABEND200 subprogram, which terminates the program and prints a storage dump.

```
 IDENTIFICATION DIVISION.
*
 PROGRAM-ID.  VSKCR.
*
 ENVIRONMENT DIVISION.
*
 INPUT-OUTPUT SECTION.
*
 FILE-CONTROL.
     SELECT INVCARDS ASSIGN TO UT-S-INVCARDS.
     SELECT INVMSTR  ASSIGN TO INVMSTR
                     ORGANIZATION IS INDEXED
                     ACCESS IS SEQUENTIAL
                     RECORD KEY IS IM-ITEM-NUMBER
                     FILE STATUS IS INVMSTR-ERROR-CODE.
*
 DATA DIVISION.
*
 FILE SECTION.
*
 FD  INVCARDS
     LABEL RECORDS ARE STANDARD
     RECORDING MODE IS F
     RECORD CONTAINS 80 CHARACTERS
     BLOCK CONTAINS 0 RECORDS.
*
 01  IC-AREA               PIC X(80).
*
 FD  INVMSTR
     LABEL RECORDS ARE STANDARD
     RECORD CONTAINS 32 CHARACTERS.
*
 01  IM-RECORD.
*
     05  IM-ITEM-NUMBER    PIC X(5).
     05  IM-ITEM-DESC      PIC X(20).
     05  IM-ON-HAND        PIC S9(5)     COMP-3.
     05  FILLER            PIC X(4).
*
 WORKING-STORAGE SECTION.
*
 01  SWITCHES.
*
     05  INVCARDS-EOF-SW       PIC X     VALUE 'N'.
         88  INVCARDS-EOF                VALUE 'Y'.
*
 01  FILE-STATUS-FIELD.
*
     05  INVMSTR-ERROR-CODE  PIC XX.
*
```

Figure 2-23 Program listing for an indexed file-creation program with complete I/O error handling (part 1 of 3)

```
 01   IC-RECORD.
*
     05   IC-ITEM-NUMBER   PIC X(5).
     05   IC-ITEM-DESC     PIC X(20).
     05   IC-ON-HAND       PIC 9(5).
     05   FILLER           PIC X(50).
*
 PROCEDURE DIVISION.
*
 000-CREATE-INVENTORY-FILE.
*
     OPEN INPUT  INVCARDS
          OUTPUT INVMSTR.
     IF INVMSTR-ERROR-CODE NOT = 00
         DISPLAY 'VSKCR  A  5  OPEN ERROR ON INVMSTR.'
         PERFORM 200-TERMINATE-LOAD-PROGRAM.
     PERFORM 100-CREATE-INVENTORY-RECORD
         UNTIL INVCARDS-EOF.
     CLOSE INVCARDS
           INVMSTR.
     IF INVMSTR-ERROR-CODE NOT = 00
         DISPLAY 'VSKCR  A  6  CLOSE ERROR ON INVMSTR.'
         PERFORM 200-TERMINATE-LOAD-PROGRAM.
     DISPLAY 'VSKCR  I  1  NORMAL EOJ'.
     STOP RUN.
*
 100-CREATE-INVENTORY-RECORD.
*
     PERFORM 110-READ-INVENTORY-RECORD.
     IF NOT INVCARDS-EOF
         MOVE IC-ITEM-NUMBER TO IM-ITEM-NUMBER
         MOVE IC-ITEM-DESC   TO IM-ITEM-DESC
         MOVE IC-ON-HAND     TO IM-ON-HAND
         PERFORM 120-WRITE-INVENTORY-RECORD.
*
 110-READ-INVENTORY-RECORD.
*
     READ INVCARDS INTO IC-RECORD
         AT END
             MOVE 'Y' TO INVCARDS-EOF-SW.
*
 120-WRITE-INVENTORY-RECORD.
*
     WRITE IM-RECORD.
     IF INVMSTR-ERROR-CODE NOT = 00
         PERFORM 130-DISPLAY-ERROR-MESSAGE.
```

Figure 2-23 Program listing for an indexed file-creation program with complete I/O error handling (part 2 of 3)

```
*
 130-DISPLAY-ERROR-MESSAGE.
*
     IF INVMSTR-ERROR-CODE = 21
         DISPLAY 'VSKCR  A  2  OUT OF SEQ RECORD--ITEM NO '
                 IM-ITEM-NUMBER '.'
     ELSE IF INVMSTR-ERROR-CODE = 22
         DISPLAY 'VSKCR  A  3  DUPLICATE KEY FOR ITEM NO '
                 IM-ITEM-NUMBER '.'
     ELSE
         DISPLAY 'VSKCR  A  4  WRITE ERROR FOR ITEM NUMBER '
                 IM-ITEM-NUMBER '.'
         PERFORM 200-TERMINATE-LOAD-PROGRAM.
*
 200-TERMINATE-LOAD-PROGRAM.
*
     DISPLAY 'VSKCR  A  8  ABENDING WITH DUMP VIA ABEND200.'
             '  FILE STATUS '  INVMSTR-ERROR-CODE  '.'.
     CALL 'ABEND200'.
```

Figure 2-23 Program listing for an indexed file-creation program with complete I/O error handling (part 3 of 3)

3

IDCAMS: The Access-Methods-Services Program

This chapter shows you how to use the VSAM utility program, IDCAMS, for basic utility functions involving key-sequenced files. Here, you will learn most of the IDCAMS functions you will ever need to use as a COBOL programmer. There are four topics in this chapter. Topic 1 presents the background information required for you to use IDCAMS. Topic 2 shows you how to use IDCAMS to define the VSAM areas required for key-sequenced files. Topic 3 shows you how to copy or print the contents of VSAM files. Topic 4 covers some of the VSAM catalog maintenance functions available with IDCAMS. Since topics 2, 3, and 4 are independent, you may read these three topics in any order you wish after you've read topic 1.

Although there are many similarities between OS and DOS IDCAMS, there are also many differences. If you are a DOS user I recommend you first read this chapter. Then, turn to the appropriate section in chapter 6 for the DOS variations. In general, you will find the majority of the DOS variations are in the job-control requirements. The IDCAMS control statements are for the most part the same.

TOPIC 1 An Introduction to Access-Methods-Services

IDCAMS is the main utility program for processing VSAM files. It is called the Access-Methods-Services program because it can perform a variety of utility services using several different access methods.

Unlike the other OS utilities, IDCAMS can process sequential files, ISAM files, or VSAM files (entry-sequenced, key-sequenced, or relative-record). The only file organization IDCAMS can't process is partitioned.

This topic presents the basics of using IDCAMS—how to set up the necessary job-control statements and how to code IDCAMS utility control statements. Then, in the next topic, I'll show you how to perform some specific utility functions using IDCAMS.

JCL requirements

Figure 3-1 illustrates the basic job-control statements needed to execute IDCAMS. As you can see, the EXEC statement identifies the utility by name (IDCAMS). Two DD statements are always required: SYSPRINT and SYSIN. The SYSPRINT DD statement tells IDCAMS where to print its messages. Usually, this DD statement is coded SYSOUT=A. The SYSIN statement is used to define the file containing the IDCAMS control statements. It is usually coded DD * to indicate that the control statements follow immediately in the job stream.

The STEPCAT DD statement is used only if you wish to use a user catalog on a VS1 system. If coded, it must be the first statement after the EXEC statement. The STEPCAT DD statement simply identifies the catalog to be used for that job step. If you wish to specify a user catalog that is to be used for all of the steps in a job, you can use a JOBCAT DD statement instead. The JOBCAT statement is coded in the same way as STEPCAT, except that it appears immediately after the JOB statement. On an MVS system, JOBCAT or STEPCAT DD statements are never required.

```
//stepname EXEC  PGM=IDCAMS
//STEPCAT   DD   step catalog (not always required)
//SYSPRINT DD   message listing (SYSOUT=A)
//ddname    DD   input or output file
//SYSIN     DD   control file (*)
        control statements
/*
```

Note: Instead of a STEPCAT DD statement, a JOBCAT DD statement may be placed immediately after the JOB statement. STEPCAT or JOBCAT is used only if you wish to override the master catalog. JOBCAT and STEPCAT are never required on an MVS system.

Figure 3-1 JCL requirements for IDCAMS

Control statements

As I have already mentioned, you must supply control statements for IDCAMS to tell it exactly what you want it to do. To code IDCAMS control statements, you must follow these rules:

1. IDCAMS control statements are coded in 80-column card format. Positions 2-72 are used for the statement and positions 73-80 may be used for optional identification or sequence numbers. Column 1 should always be blank.
2. All IDCAMS control statements follow this general pattern:

   ```
   command parameters ...
   ```

   The command specifies the operation to be performed. The parameters provide information needed by IDCAMS to perform the specified operation.
3. Parameters are separated by a space or a comma. In all of the examples in this book, I separate the parameters with spaces. However, if you feel more comfortable using commas, by all means use them. Both are acceptable.
4. To specify a parameter's value, each parameter name is immediately followed by its value enclosed in parentheses. Here's an example:

   ```
   NAME(H4$.ARMST)
   ```
5. To continue a statement on the next line, code a hyphen (-) after a parameter and begin the next parameter on the next line. The hyphen may be preceded by a space for readability. Here's an example:

   ```
   FILE(LIBAREA) -
   VOLUME(USER20)
   ```

   No special character is required in position 72 to indicate a continuation line.
6. Comments may be included anywhere in the IDCAMS control statements. An IDCAMS comment string begins with the characters /* and ends with */. Here's an example of a comment:

   ```
   KEY(50) /* ITEM NUMBER */
   ```

Discussion

Although the IBM manual documents 23 IDCAMS control statements with literally hundreds of possible operands, I'm only going to cover a few of them in this book. In the next three topics, I will show you how to use IDCAMS control statements to define a data space and a key-sequenced cluster, to copy or print a key-sequenced file, and to perform routine VSAM catalog maintenance. Other features of IDCAMS will be presented in the remaining chapters of this book when needed. The IDCAMS statements that aren't covered in this book are rarely used.

If you feel overwhelmed by the long list of coding rules for IDCAMS control statements, relax. It isn't that complex at all. In fact, most of the time it's easier to code IDCAMS control statements than it is to code control statements for the other OS utility programs. In any event, you'll see enough examples of IDCAMS control statements in the next topic and throughout this book that you should have no difficulty coding them yourself.

Objectives

1. Identify the JCL statements required to execute the IDCAMS utility.
2. List the coding rules for IDCAMS control statements.

TOPIC 2 Defining VSAM Areas with IDCAMS

Before you can load and use a VSAM file, you must do three things. First, you must find out how the file is to be defined: what user catalog will contain the cluster's entry, what volume the file will be placed on, what the name of the file will be, how much space will be allocated to the file, and so on. Second, you must make sure that the volume that will contain the file has enough VSAM space available. Usually, this will be taken care of by systems programmers, but in some cases you may have to create the VSAM space yourself. Third, you must define the cluster itself. To define VSAM space and clusters through IDCAMS, you use the DEFINE statement.

Defining a data space

As I have already said, systems programmers are generally responsible for managing VSAM data space. However, this isn't always so. In some cases, you may be asked to define a VSAM file on a volume that contains no VSAM space, so you must define the space yourself. There are two ways to define VSAM space. One is to use the DEFINE SPACE statement, which I will describe in just a moment. The other way is to define the space at the same time you define the cluster. I'll describe this technique in the section on defining a cluster.

The DEFINE SPACE statement is shown in figure 3-2. As you can see, the DEFINE SPACE statement has several parameters. The first one, FILE, identifies the ddname of a DD statement that defines the volume that will contain the data space. The next parameter, VOLUMES, names the volume defined by the DD statement specified in the FILE parameter.

The next parameter of the DEFINE SPACE statement is used to tell IDCAMS how large the data space is going to be. The space may be allocated in terms of cylinders, tracks, or records. In addition, you may specify two types of allocation: primary and secondary. As a general rule, the *primary allocation* should be the amount of space you think the file will require. This is the amount of space initially allocated to the data space.

However, estimates can be wrong and file sizes do change. As a result, the *secondary allocation* allows for extensions to the primary allocation. Then, if the primary allocation of space isn't large enough, the secondary allocation is made. If this still isn't enough space, the secondary allocation is repeated until a total of 15 secondary extents have been added to the data space.

Figure 3-3 shows three examples of the allocation parameter. In example 1, the primary allocation and secondary allocation are both one cylinder. If one cylinder isn't enough to hold the data in the space, another cylinder will be allocated. If that isn't enough space

The DEFINE SPACE statement

```
DEFINE SPACE -
        (FILE(ddname) -
          VOLUMES(vol-ser) -

         {RECORDS  }
         {TRACKS   }  (primary secondary)
         {CYLINDERS}

          RECORDSIZE (average maximum))
```

Explanation

FILE	The name of a DD statement that identifies the volume that will contain the data space.
VOLUMES	The volume serial number of the volume that will contain the data space.
{RECORDS / TRACKS / CYLINDERS}	The space allocation for the data space. RECORDS, TRACKS, or CYLINDERS specifies the unit of allocation. Primary specifies how many units to allocate initially, and secondary specifies the secondary allocation in case the primary space becomes full.
RECORDSIZE	The average and maximum record size.

Figure 3-2 The DEFINE SPACE statement

Example 1

```
CYLINDERS(1 1)
```

Example 2

```
TRACKS(5 2)
```

Example 3

```
RECORDS(5000 500) -
RECORDSIZE(100 100)
```

Figure 3-3 Examples of the space allocation parameter for the DEFINE SPACE statement

for the data, another cylinder will be added, and so on until 15 secondary allocations have been made. So the total possible allocation for this data space is 16 cylinders.

Example 2 provides for a primary allocation of five tracks and a secondary allocation of two tracks. Thus, if the data cannot be stored in the five tracks initially allocated, additional tracks will be allocated, two at a time, until a total of 15 two-track areas have been added to the primary amount. So the total possible allocation for this data space is 35 tracks.

Example 3 shows how space can be allocated in terms of records. Here, the primary allocation is 5000 records and the secondary allocation is 500 records. When you code the RECORDS form of the allocation parameter, you must also code the RECORDSIZE parameter. The RECORDSIZE parameter specifies two values: the maximum record length and the average record length. For fixed-length records, these two values will be the same. For variable-length records, they will be different. In the example, the records are a fixed length of 100 bytes.

Figure 3-4 illustrates a job to define a data space on a 3330 volume named VSAMC1. The DEFINE statement specifies that 400 cylinders are to be allocated for VSAM; since a 3330 disk pack contains 400 cylinders, this DEFINE statement specifies that the entire volume is to be reserved for VSAM files.

Defining a cluster

After a data space has been allocated on a direct-access volume, you can define a cluster. A second variation of the DEFINE statement,

```
//H4VS3$4   JOB   (0642,VSAMXXXXX,BD,201),
//                'DOUG LOWE'
//          EXEC   PGM=IDCAMS
//SYSPRINT  DD   SYSOUT=A
//VSAMC1    DD   UNIT=3330,
//               VOL=SER=VSAMC1,
//               DISP=OLD
//SYSIN     DD   *
 DEFINE SPACE -
          (FILE(VSAMC1) -
            VOLUMES(VSAMC1) -
            CYLINDERS(400) )
/*
```

Figure 3-4 Defining a VSAM data space

the DEFINE CLUSTER statement, is used for this purpose. The DEFINE CLUSTER statement is illustrated in figure 3-5.

The overall structure of the DEFINE CLUSTER statement is this:

```
DEFINE CLUSTER -
  (parameters)...  -
  DATA -
    parameters...  -
  INDEX -
    parameters...
```

The first set of parameters is used to specify attributes that apply to the entire cluster. The next set of parameters (following the keyword DATA) specifies attributes that apply only to the data component of the cluster; the third set of parameters (following INDEX) applies only to the index component. Although the IBM manual documents about 30 parameters for each component group (DATA and INDEX), I have only included the NAME parameter here because the others aren't frequently used.

The first parameter of the DEFINE CLUSTER statement is the name of the VSAM data set being defined. This is the name that will be used in the DSNAME parameter of the DD statement to access the file later. The NAME parameter may be coded with qualification, as in this example:

```
NAME(H4$.RETAIL.OPENITEM)
```

On an MVS system, the first node (in this case, H4$) must be the name of a valid user catalog, unless the cluster is to be cataloged in the master catalog.

The NAME parameters for the DATA and INDEX components are used to assign meaningful names to the DATA and INDEX com-

The DEFINE CLUSTER statement

```
DEFINE CLUSTER -
        (NAME(cluster-name) -
          VOLUMES(vol-ser) -
          {RECORDS  }
          {TRACKS   }  (primary secondary) -
          {CYLINDERS}
          RECORDSIZE(average maximum) -
          INDEXED -
          KEYS(length offset) -
          UNIQUE -
          FILE(ddname) -
          MODEL(cluster-name) ) -
        DATA -
          NAME(entry-name) -
        INDEX -
          NAME(entry-name)
```

Figure 3-5 The DEFINE CLUSTER statement (part 1 of 2)

ponents of the cluster. This can be helpful when reading catalog or VTOC listings. A good way to form the data or index component name is to suffix the cluster name with .DATA or .INDEX. Thus, the DATA and INDEX NAME parameters for the previous example could be coded like this:

```
DATA -
  NAME(H4$.RETAIL.OPENITEM.DATA) -
INDEX -
  NAME(H4$.RETAIL.OPENITEM.INDEX)
```

If the DATA and INDEX NAME parameters are omitted, the system will generate long and meaningless names (you can see examples of the names generated by the system in figure 3-16).

Explanation

NAME	The name assigned to the cluster, data component, or index component.
VOLUMES	The volume serial number of the volume that will contain this cluster.
{RECORDS / TRACKS / CYLINDERS}	The space allocation for the cluster. RECORDS, TRACKS, or CYLINDERS specifies the unit of allocation. Primary specifies the number of units to be allocated initially, and secondary specifies the secondary allocation in case the primary space becomes full.
RECORDSIZE	The average and maximum record size.
INDEXED	Key-sequenced file organization.
KEYS	The length and offset of the record key.
UNIQUE	Specifies that a data space should be created for this cluster.
FILE	Specifies the ddname of a DD statement that defines the volume that will contain the data space. Required only if UNIQUE is coded.
MODEL	Specifies the name of a VSAM cluster on which this cluster is to be modeled; values for parameters not included in this DEFINE statement will be derived from the model cluster.

Figure 3-5 The DEFINE CLUSTER statement (part 2 of 2)

The VOLUMES parameter provides the name of the volume that will contain the cluster. Then, the allocation parameter specifies how much space is to be allocated for the cluster. Like the allocation for a data space, the allocation for a cluster is given in primary and secondary amounts. Again, up to 15 secondary extents will be allocated before the file runs out of space. The RECORDSIZE parameter is always required; it specifies the average and maximum record lengths for the records in the cluster.

The INDEXED parameter is always required for a key-sequenced file. It is followed by the KEYS parameter, which specifies the length and offset of the file's record key (the first byte of the record is offset 0). If the record key is in position 4-8, you would code the KEYS parameter like this:

```
KEYS(5 3)
```

Here, the KEYS parameter specifies that the key is five bytes long and is offset three bytes from the first byte of the record.

UNIQUE and FILE are used to define a cluster on a volume that doesn't already contain a VSAM data space. When UNIQUE and

FILE are coded, a data space is automatically generated on the specified volume. The data space may contain only the cluster being defined; it can't contain any other clusters. A DD statement defining the volume must be included in the job stream if UNIQUE and FILE are coded.

The MODEL parameter is used to specify that default parameter values are to be taken from an existing cluster. When MODEL is coded, any parameters not coded in the DEFINE CLUSTER statement will be taken from the model cluster. This is often used to establish installation standards for things like control interval size, index size, and so on. In many cases, systems programmers create model clusters with critical parameters set to the most efficient values. If such model clusters are available to you, by all means use them.

Figure 3-6 shows an example of a job that defines a key-sequenced file. Notice that no DD statement is required to indicate the volume that will contain the file. The DEFINE CLUSTER statement specifies that the file name will be H4$.INVMSTR, the volume is VSAMC1, the primary allocation is 100 records and the secondary allocation is 30 records, the records are a fixed length of 32 bytes, and the key is five bytes long beginning in byte 1 (offset 0) of the record.

Figure 3-7 illustrates a job that defines an indexed file on a volume that contains no data space. Here, a DD statement is required to define the volume that will contain the data space and the file. The DEFINE CLUSTER statement in figure 3-7 is the same as the one in figure 3-6 except that the UNIQUE and FILE parameters are coded.

```
//H4VS3$6   JOB   (0642,VSAMXXXXX,BD,201),
//                'DOUG LOWE'
//          EXEC   PGM=IDCAMS
//SYSPRINT DD   SYSOUT=A
//SYSIN     DD   *
 DEFINE CLUSTER -
          (NAME(H4$.INVMSTR) -
            VOLUMES(VSAMC1) -
            RECORDS(100 30) -
            RECORDSIZE(32 32) -
            INDEXED -
            KEYS(5 0) ) -
          DATA -
            NAME(H4$.INVMSTR.DATA) -
          INDEX -
            NAME(H4$.INVMSTR.INDEX)
/*
```

Figure 3-6 Defining a key-sequenced cluster

```
//H4VS3$7   JOB   (0642,VSAMXXXXX,BD,201),
//               'DOUG LOWE'
//          EXEC   PGM=IDCAMS
//SYSPRINT  DD   SYSOUT=A
//VSAMC1    DD   UNIT=SYSDA,
//               VOL=SER=VSAMC1,
//               DISP=OLD
//SYSIN     DD   *
 DEFINE CLUSTER -
           (NAME(H4$.INVMSTR) -
             VOLUMES(VSAMC1) -
             RECORDS(100 30) -
             RECORDSIZE(32 32) -
             INDEXED -
             KEYS(5 0) -
             UNIQUE -
             FILE(VSAMC1) ) -
           DATA -
             NAME(H4$.INVMSTR.DATA) -
           INDEX -
             NAME(H4$.INVMSTR.INDEX)
/*
```

Figure 3-7 Defining a unique key-sequenced file

Discussion

At this point, you may be thinking that a lot of unnecessary effort is required just to establish a VSAM file. But when you look at it more closely, you will see that it is actually easier to define a VSAM key-sequenced data set using IDCAMS than it is to create an ISAM file using OS JCL. Under VSAM, you usually don't have to worry about things like the blocking factor, how many tracks to reserve for the index, and other details. If you omit a parameter, VSAM will usually choose a default value for you. And if a model cluster is used, efficient defaults can be provided by a previously defined cluster.

Terminology

primary allocation

secondary allocation

Objectives

1. Given a problem involving the definition of a VSAM area, code the appropriate JCL and control statements for its solution.

TOPIC 3 Copying and Printing With IDCAMS

Two common utility functions performed by IDCAMS are copying and printing files. IDCAMS can copy or print VSAM or non-VSAM files. For copy operations, the REPRO statement is used; for print operations, the PRINT statement is used. This topic shows you how to use both statements.

Copying files

All of IDCAMS' copy operations are done using the REPRO statement. The syntax of the REPRO statement is illustrated in figure 3-8. As you can see, REPRO requires only two parameters. INFILE specifies a DD statement that defines the input file, and OUTFILE specifies the DD statement for the output file.

IDCAMS allows any arrangement of VSAM and non-VSAM files for its copy operations. You can copy a VSAM file to another VSAM file, you can copy a non-VSAM file to a VSAM file, or you can copy a VSAM file to a non-VSAM file. The only restriction is that if the output file is non-VSAM, it must be sequential—it can't be ISAM or direct.

Figure 3-9 shows a job that copies a VSAM file named H4$.INVMSTR. The output is another VSAM file named H4$.INVMSTR2. Since the output file is a VSAM file, it must be defined previously with a DEFINE statement. That's why the INVMSTR2 DD statement specifies DISP=OLD.

Figure 3-10 shows an IDCAMS job that loads a VSAM file from a non-VSAM file. Here, the input file is defined in the JCL as H4.INVMSTR.DATA, and the output file is a VSAM file named H4$.INVMSTR. The input file's organization may be sequential or ISAM; in either case, IDCAMS converts the file to a key-sequenced

The REPRO statement

```
REPRO INFILE(ddname) -
      OUTFILE(ddname)
```

Explanation

INFILE	Identifies the input file's DD statement.
OUTFILE	Identifies the output file's DD statement.

Figure 3-8 The REPRO statement

```
//H4VS3$9   JOB   (0642,VSAMXXXXX,BD,201),
//                'DOUG LOWE'
//          EXEC   PGM=IDCAMS
//SYSPRINT DD   SYSOUT=A
//INVMSTR  DD   DSN=H4$.INVMSTR,
//              DISP=OLD
//INVMSTR2 DD   DSN=H4$.INVMSTR2,
//              DISP=OLD
//SYSIN    DD   *
 REPRO INFILE(INVMSTR) -
       OUTFILE(INVMSTR2)
/*
```

Figure 3-9 Copying a VSAM file

```
//H4VS3$10 JOB   (0642,VSAMXXXXX,BD,201),
//                'DOUG LOWE'
//          EXEC   PGM=IDCAMS
//SYSPRINT DD   SYSOUT=A
//INVMSTR  DD   DSN=H4$.INVMSTR,
//              DISP=OLD
//INDD     DD   DSN=H4$.INVMSTR.DATA,
//              UNIT=SYSDA,
//              DISP=OLD
//SYSIN    DD   *
 REPRO INFILE(INDD) -
       OUTFILE(INVMSTR)
/*
```

Figure 3-10 Loading a VSAM file from a non-VSAM file

VSAM file (assuming that's how H4$.INVMSTR was defined). If the input file is ISAM, dummy records (records which have been logically deleted, indicated by hex FF in the first byte of the record) are automatically deleted from the file as it is copied.

Figure 3-11 shows a job that copies a VSAM file to a non-VSAM file. Here, the JCL defines the input file as a VSAM file named H4$.INVMSTR, and the output file as a new sequential file named H4$.INVMSTR.BACKUP. Remember that a non-VSAM output file must be sequential—ISAM is not allowed.

Printing files

The PRINT statement, shown in figure 3-12, is used for all IDCAMS printing operations. As you can see, its format is simple. INFILE

```
//H4VS3$11 JOB   (0642,VSAMXXXXX,BD,201),
//                'DOUG LOWE'
//             EXEC   PGM=IDCAMS
//SYSPRINT DD   SYSOUT=A
//INVMSTR   DD   DSN=H4$.INVMSTR,
//                DISP=OLD
//OUTDD     DD   DSN=H4$.INVMSTR.BACKUP,
//                DISP=(NEW,KEEP),
//                UNIT=SYSDA,
//                VOL=SER=OSTR27,
//                DCB=(RECFM=FB,LRECL=32,BLKSIZE=3200),
//                SPACE=(CYL,(20,15))
//SYSIN     DD   *
 REPRO INFILE(INVMSTR) -
       OUTFILE(OUTDD)
/*
```

Figure 3-11 Copying a VSAM file to a non-VSAM file

The PRINT statement

```
PRINT INFILE(ddname) -

        {CHARACTER}
        {HEX      }
        {DUMP     }
```

Explanation

INFILE	Identifies the DD statement for the input file.
{CHARACTER / HEX / DUMP}	Specifies the format of the listing. CHARACTER prints a straight listing of the file; HEX converts the data to hexadecimal notation before printing; and DUMP prints both character and hex formats. If omitted, DUMP is assumed.

Figure 3-12 The PRINT statement

specifies the ddname of the input file. Coding CHARACTER, HEX, or DUMP specifies the format of the printed output. (DUMP is the default if no format is coded.) If CHARACTER is specified, the output is printed exactly as it appears in the input record. If HEX is specified, each character is converted to a two-character hexadecimal code before printing. If DUMP is coded, the output is printed in both forms, much like a storage dump.

To illustrate the use of the PRINT statement, consider figure 3-13. Although a VSAM file is printed in this example, a non-VSAM

The JCL

```
//H4VS3$13 JOB  (0642,VSAMXXXXX,BD,201),
//              'DOUG LOWE'
//          EXEC  PGM=IDCAMS
//SYSPRINT DD   SYSOUT=A
//INVMSTR  DD   DSN=H4$.INVMSTR,
//              DISP=OLD
//SYSIN    DD   *
 PRINT INFILE(INVMSTR) -
       CHARACTER
/*
```

Resulting output

```
IDCAMS  SYSTEM SERVICES


LISTING OF DATA SET -H4$.INVMSTR

KEY OF RECORD - 00101
001013800 PROC 64K          ...

KEY OF RECORD - 00102
001023800 PROC 128K         .."

KEY OF RECORD - 00103
001033810 PROC 64K          ...

KEY OF RECORD - 00104
001043810 PROC 128K         ...

KEY OF RECORD - 00105
001053820 PROC 64K          ...

KEY OF RECORD - 00106
001063820 PROC 128K         ...
 .
 .
 .
KEY OF RECORD - 00300
003001800 PROC 64K          ...

KEY OF RECORD - 00301
003011800 PROC 128K         ...

IDC0005I NUMBER OF RECORDS PROCESSED WAS 15

IDC0001I FUNCTION COMPLETED, HIGHEST CONDITION CODE WAS 0
```

Figure 3-13 Printing a VSAM file in CHARACTER format

file (sequential or ISAM) can be printed by IDCAMS as well. The bottom part of this figure shows how the output appears for a VSAM key-sequenced file. (The dots in the output portion of figure 3-13 represent unprintable characters—in this case, a packed-decimal number.)

Figure 3-14 is a listing of the same file produced with the DUMP option. Here, the left-hand side of the listing gives a hexadecimal listing of the data. On the right, the data is printed in character format. Because this format takes more room than the CHARACTER format, I recommend you use it only when you must.

Discussion

I hope you can appreciate the flexibility that IDCAMS provides in terms of the combinations of input and output file types that are allowed for copy and print operations. You should realize, however, that IDCAMS doesn't allow you to modify the contents of records as they are copied or printed, as you can with the standard OS utilities. So in order to copy a VSAM file with record modifications, you must first copy it to a non-VSAM file (sequential), make the modifications using a utility like IEBGENER, and re-copy the file to VSAM.

Objectives

1. Given a problem that involves copying or printing a VSAM or non-VSAM file, code an IDCAMS job for its solution.

TOPIC 4 IDCAMS Catalog Maintenance Functions

This topic shows you how to use a few of the IDCAMS catalog maintenance functions. First, I will show you how to use the LISTCAT statement to list the contents of a VSAM catalog. Then, I will show you how to perform various catalog maintenance functions such as deleting files, renaming files, and cataloging non-VSAM files.

Listing a VSAM catalog

Figure 3-15 shows the format of the LISTCAT statement, which is used to list the contents of a VSAM catalog. As you can see, you

```
IDCAMS  SYSTEM SERVICES

LISTING OF DATA SET -H4$.INVMSTR

KEY OF RECORD - F0F0F1F0F1
000000  F0F0F1F0 F1F3F8F0 F040D7D9 D6C340F6  F4D24040 40404040 4000000F 40404040  *001013800 PROC 64K     ...  *

KEY OF RECORD - F0F0F1F0F2
000000  F0F0F1F0 F2F3F8F0 F040D7D9 D6C340F1  F2F8D240 40404040 4000007F 40404040  *001023800 PROC 128K    .."  *

KEY OF RECORD - F0F0F1F0F3
000000  F0F0F1F0 F3F3F8F1 F040D7D9 D6C340F6  F4D24040 40404040 4000002F 40404040  *001033810 PROC 64K     ...  *

KEY OF RECORD - F0F0F1F0F4
000000  F0F0F1F0 F4F3F8F1 F040D7D9 D6C340F1  F2F8D240 40404040 4000009F 40404040  *001043810 PROC 128K    ...  *
.
.
.
KEY OF RECORD - F0F0F2F1F0
000000  F0F0F2F1 F0C1C3E3 C9E5C540 C8E4C240  40404040 40404040 4000030F 40404040  *00210ACTIVE HUB       ...  *

KEY OF RECORD - F0F0F2F1F1
000000  F0F0F2F1 F1D7C1E2 E2C9E5C5 40C8E4C2  40404040 40404040 4000150F 40404040  *00211PASSIVE HUB      ...  *

KEY OF RECORD - F0F0F2F5F0
000000  F0F0F2F5 F0C3C1C2 D3C540F1 F0F0C6E3  40404040 40404040 4000050F 40404040  *00250CABLE 100FT      ...  *

KEY OF RECORD - F0F0F3F0F0
000000  F0F0F3F0 F0F1F8F0 F040D7D9 D6C340F6  F4D24040 40404040 4000003F 40404040  *003001800 PROC 64K     ...  *

IDC0005I NUMBER OF RECORDS PROCESSED WAS 15

IDC0001I FUNCTION COMPLETED, HIGHEST CONDITION CODE WAS 0
```

Figure 3-14 Printout of a VSAM file in DUMP format

The LISTCAT statement

```
LISTCAT CATALOG(catalog-name) -
        ENTRIES(name...) -
        type -

        {NAME  }
        {VOLUME}
        {ALL   }
```

Explanation

CATALOG	Specifies the name of the catalog to be listed. If omitted, the master catalog or the catalog specified in a JOBCAT or STEPCAT statement is used.
ENTRIES	Specifies the names of entries to be listed. If omitted, all entries are listed.
type	Specifies the type of entries to be listed. If omitted, all types of entries are listed. Possible values are: CLUSTER, DATA, INDEX, NONVSAM, and SPACE. (See the IBM manual for other values.)
{NAME / VOLUME / ALL}	Specifies what information is to be listed. NAME lists the name and type of each entry. VOLUME lists the name, entry type, owner-id, creation and expiration dates, and the volume containing the file. ALL lists all the fields for each entry. (See the IBM manual for other values that may be coded here.)

Figure 3-15 The LISTCAT statement

may code several parameters. The first, CATALOG, specifies the name of the catalog to be listed. If CATALOG is omitted, the master catalog or the JOBCAT or STEPCAT catalog is listed.

The next two parameters, ENTRIES and type, are used to specify that only certain catalog entries are to be listed. If ENTRIES is coded, it specifies the names of the catalog entries to be listed. If type is coded, it specifies that only certain types of catalog entries are to be listed (such as clusters, non-VSAM, indexed, etc.). If no type is specified, all entries are listed.

The last parameter specifies the information that is to be printed for each entry. If you specify NAME, only the name and entry type of each entry is listed. If you specify VOLUME, IDCAMS lists the name, entry type, owner-id, creation and expiration dates, and the volume containing the file. If you code ALL, all of the fields stored in the catalog entry are listed. You may code many other values here as well, but NAME, VOLUME, and ALL are the most useful.

Figure 3-16 shows a job that lists the contents of a VSAM catalog. Here, all of the cluster entries in the catalog are listed with the NAME format. The bottom part of the figure shows the output

The JCL

```
//H4VS3$16 JOB  (0642,VSAMXXXXX,BD,201),
//              'DOUG LOWE'
//           EXEC  PGM=IDCAMS
//SYSPRINT DD  SYSOUT=A
//SYSIN     DD  *
 LISTCAT CLUSTER -
         NAME
/*
```

Resulting output

```
IDCAMS  SYSTEM SERVICES

 LISTCAT CLUSTER -
         NAME
CLUSTER ------- H4$.ARTRANS
     IN-CAT --- SYSV.VSAMC1
   DATA ------- VSAMDSET.T9623CA0.DFD80304.T90FE2C2.T9623CA0
     IN-CAT --- SYSC.VSAMC1
CLUSTER ------- H4$.EOSMAS
     IN-CAT --- SYSV.VSAMC1
   DATA ------- VSAMDSET.TD61F310.DFD80304.T90FE2C3.TD61F310
     IN-CAT --- SYSV.VSAMC1
CLUSTER ------- H4$.ITRAN2
     IN-CAT --- SYSV.VSAMC1
   DATA ------- VSAMDSET.TD428050.DFD80304.T90FE2BA.TD428050
     IN-CAT --- SYSV.VSAMC1
CLUSTER ------- H4$.ARMAST
     IN-CAT --- SYSV.VSAMC1
   DATA ------- VSAMDSET.T5119310.DFD80304.T90FE2BC.T5119310
     IN-CAT --- SYSV.VSAMC1
   INDEX ------ VSAMDSET.T5119790.DFD80304.T90FE2BC.T5119790
     IN-CAT --- SYSV.VSAMC1
CLUSTER ------- H4$.TJKKMST
     IN-CAT --- SYSV.VSAMC1
   DATA ------- VSAMDSET.TACED1A0.DFD80304.T90FE2C0.TACED1A0
     IN-CAT --- SYSV.VSAMC1
   INDEX ------ VSAMDSET.TACED630.DFD80304.T90FE2C0.TACED630
     IN-CAT --- SYSV.VSAMC1
```

Figure 3-16 Listing a VSAM catalog

generated by this job. As you can see, the listing isn't very easy to read. For each VSAM data set, the listing shows the cluster name and the name of the elements containing the data and index. In addition, the listing shows the catalog containing the entry for each element (SYSV.VSAMC1 for each element listed in figure 3-16).

Maintaining catalogs

VSAM catalog maintenance is performed by IDCAMS using three statements: DELETE, ALTER, and DEFINE NONVSAM. These are illustrated in figure 3-17. The DELETE statement is used primarily to remove entries from a VSAM catalog. The ALTER statement is used to change entries. DEFINE NONVSAM is used to enter non-VSAM files into the VSAM catalog.

Figure 3-18 shows an IDCAMS job that uses the DELETE statement to delete several catalog entries. The first DELETE statement simply specifies that all entries made under the name H4$.ITRAN2 should be deleted. The second DELETE statement says to delete only the cluster entry for a file named H4$.TRCMS. The last DELETE statement tells IDCAMS to remove the entry for a non-VSAM file named H4.ARMAST from the VSAM catalog. The SCRATCH parameter says to remove H4.ARMAST from the VTOC as well. If SCRATCH isn't coded, the non-VSAM file would simply be uncataloged.

Figure 3-19 shows how the ALTER command can be used to change the name of a VSAM data set. Here, the first parameter specifies the old name of the file (H4$.INVTRAN), and the NEWNAME parameter specifies the new file name (H4$.ICTRAN). Although the ALTER command has dozens of subparameters, it is beyond the scope of this book to cover them here. So if you need to change any item in a catalog entry other than the entry name, consult the IBM manual to determine the correct parameter.

Figure 3-20 shows how the DEFINE NONVSAM command is used to enter a non-VSAM file into a VSAM catalog. Here, the file name is H4.BJTRAN, the device type is SYSDA, and the volume name is OSTR32. Once a non-VSAM file is entered into a VSAM catalog, you only need to specify DSNAME and DISP=OLD to access it.

Discussion

This has of course been a brief introduction to the catalog maintenance functions available with IDCAMS. I have only covered the basic functions you are likely to require. If you need to do more advanced catalog maintenance functions, consult the IBM manuals.

One other point: whenever you are performing catalog maintenance functions, be sure to follow the standards established by your installation. If, for example, your installation has a rule against cataloging non-VSAM files in a user catalog, don't do it.

Objectives

1. Given a problem involving VSAM catalog maintenance, code an acceptable IDCAMS job for its solution.

The DELETE statement

```
DELETE (entry-name...) -
          type -
          SCRATCH
```

Explanation

entry–name	Specifies the names of the entries to be deleted.
type	Specifies the type of entries to be deleted. Possible values are CLUSTER, SPACE, NONVSAM. (See the IBM manual for other values.)
SCRATCH	Indicates that a NONVSAM file should be scratched from the VTOC as well as from the VSAM catalog.

The ALTER statement

```
ALTER entry-name -
         NEWNAME(new-name)
```

Explanation

entry–name	Specifies the name of the entry to be altered.
NEWNAME	Specifies a new name for the entry.

Note: There are many other options for the ALTER statement, but NEWNAME is the most commonly used.

The DEFINE NONVSAM statement

```
DEFINE NONVSAM
        (NAME(entry-name) -
         DEVICETYPES(device-type) -
         VOLUMES(vol-ser)
```

Explanation

NAME	Specifies the data set name of the non-VSAM file to be cataloged.
DEVICETYPES	Specifies the device type (UNIT) of the file.
VOLUMES	Specifies the volume serial number of the volume containing the file.

Figure 3-17 IDCAMS catalog maintenance statements

```
//H4VS3$18 JOB   (0642,VSAMXXXXX,BD,201),
//               'DOUG LOWE'
//           EXEC   PGM=IDCAMS
//SYSPRINT DD   SYSOUT=A
//SYSIN     DD   *
 DELETE (H4$.ITRAN2)
 DELETE (H4$.TRCMS) -
           CLUSTER
 DELETE (H4.ARMAST) -
           SCRATCH
/*
```

Figure 3-18 Deleting VSAM catalog entries

```
//H4VS3$19 JOB   (0642,VSAMXXXXX,BD,201),
//               'DOUG LOWE'
//           EXEC   PGM=IDCAMS
//SYSPRINT DD   SYSOUT=A
//SYSIN     DD   *
 ALTER (H4$.INVTRAN) -
           NEWNAME(H4$.ICTRAN)
/*
```

Figure 3-19 Renaming a VSAM file

```
//H4VS3$20 JOB   (0642,VSAMXXXXX,BD,201),
//               'DOUG LOWE'
//           EXEC   PGM=IDCAMS
//SYSPRINT DD   SYSOUT=A
//SYSIN     DD   *
 DEFINE NONVSAM -
         (NAME(H$.BJTRAN) -
           DEVICETYPES(SYSDA) -
           VOLUMES(OSTR32) )
/*
```

Figure 3-20 Cataloging a non-VSAM file in a VSAM catalog

PART THREE

Other VSAM File Organizations

Although most VSAM files are key-sequenced, VSAM allows two other file organizations as well: entry-sequenced and relative-record. The two chapters in this part show you how to process these types of files. Chapter 4 presents what you need to know to process entry-sequenced VSAM files, including the COBOL elements and IDCAMS requirements. Chapter 5 presents the requirements for relative-record files. Since DOS VSAM does not provide for relative-record files, DOS users may ignore chapter 5.

TOD CLOCK
SECURE
POWER OFF
ENABLE SET
DATA
LOAD UNIT ADDRESS
E
D
REGISTER
ZONE
AUXILIARY/WORK STORAGE
LOAD
SYS
MAN
WAIT
TEST
LOAD

4

Processing Entry-Sequenced Files

This chapter shows you how to process VSAM entry-sequenced files. An entry-sequenced file is similar to a non-VSAM sequential file. The records in the file are accessed in the order in which they were loaded. Additions are always made at the end of the file.

In order to process an entry-sequenced file, you must know three things. First, you must know how to code the correct COBOL statements to process the file. Second, you must know how to code IDCAMS control statements to define, copy, and print the file. And third, you must know how to code the JCL statements used to process the file. This chapter presents this information in terms of OS VSAM; DOS users should first read this chapter and then read chapter 6 for DOS variations.

COBOL REQUIREMENTS

Figure 4-1 summarizes the COBOL elements used to process VSAM entry-sequenced files. In general, these elements are the same as the ones used to process standard sequential files. The entries in figure 4-1 that differ from those used for standard sequential files are shaded.

To show you how these elements are actually used, a simple file-to-printer program is illustrated in figures 4-2 and 4-3. Figure 4-2 is a structure chart for this program and, as you can see, the printed output requires no headings, page overflow, or final totals. This will let

```
IDENTIFICATION DIVISION.
    .
    .
ENVIRONMENT DIVISION.
    .
    .
INPUT-OUTPUT SECTION.
FILE-CONTROL.
    SELECT file-name ASSIGN TO assignment-name
        [ORGANIZATION IS SEQUENTIAL]
        [ACCESS MODE IS SEQUENTIAL
        [FILE STATUS IS data-name]
    .
    .
DATA DIVISION.
FILE SECTION.
FD  file-name
    LABEL RECORDS ARE STANDARD
    RECORD CONTAINS integer CHARACTERS
    [BLOCK CONTAINS integer RECORDS].
    .
    .
Note: The RECORDING MODE clause is invalid for VSAM files.

PROCEDURE DIVISION.

         {INPUT  file-name ...}
    OPEN {OUTPUT file-name ...} ...
         {EXTEND file-name ...}

    READ file-name RECORD
        [INTO data-name]
        AT END imperative-statement.

    WRITE record-name
        [FROM data-name] .

Note: The INVALID KEY clause is invalid for entry-sequenced VSAM files.

    CLOSE file-name ...
```

Figure 4-1 COBOL elements for processing entry-sequenced files

you concentrate on the coding for the VSAM file. The complete listing for this program is given in figure 4-3. The shaded portions of figure 4-3 indicate the coding entries required for VSAM.

The Environment Division

The SELECT statement for a VSAM entry-sequenced file is somewhat different than the one for a key-sequenced file. To begin with, the ORGANIZATION is SEQUENTIAL rather than INDEXED. And

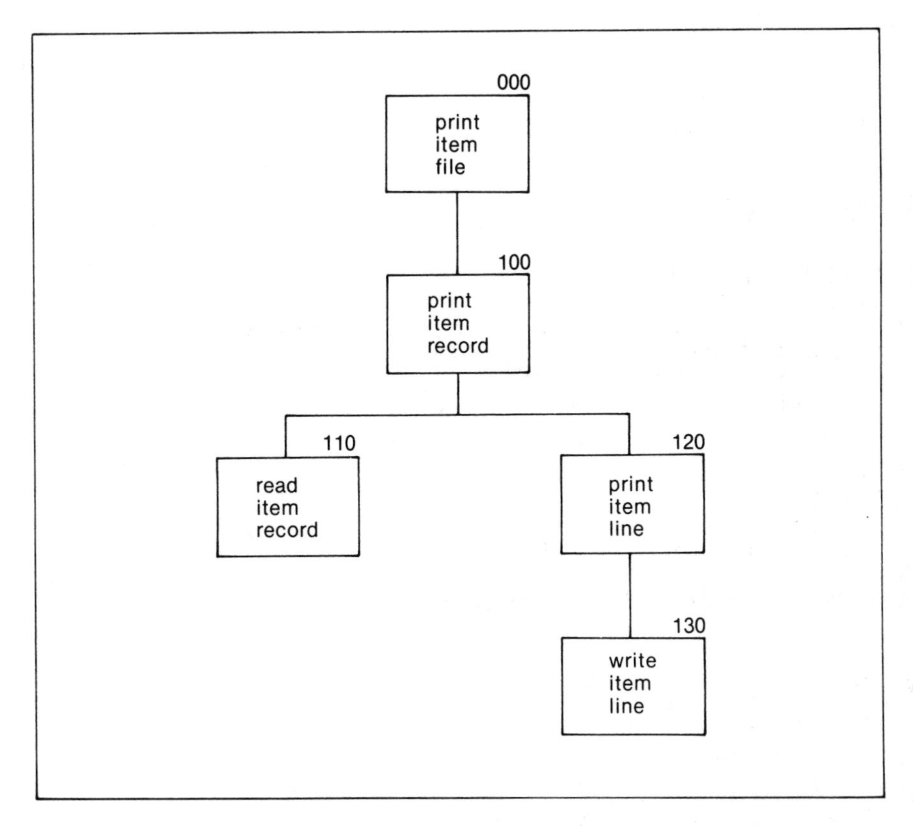

Figure 4-2 Structure chart for the entry-sequenced file-to-printer program

the ACCESS mode is always SEQUENTIAL; random access is not possible with an entry-sequenced file. The FILE STATUS field is used just the same as it is for key-sequenced files. And, of course, the RECORD KEY clause is not used for entry-sequenced files.

The assignment name in the ASSIGN clause is a little different than the one used for key-sequenced files. The one for entry-sequenced files has this format:

```
comment-AS-ddname
```

The AS is required to indicate that the file is a VSAM sequential file (S is coded for non-VSAM sequential files).

The Data Division

The FD statement for a VSAM entry-sequenced file is the same as the FD statement for a VSAM indexed file. The LABEL RECORDS clause, though always required, is treated as documentation no matter how you code it; the RECORDING MODE clause is invalid for VSAM files; and the BLOCK CONTAINS clause is treated as documentation and may be omitted.

```
 IDENTIFICATION DIVISION.
*
 PROGRAM-ID.  VSELST.
*
 ENVIRONMENT DIVISION.
*
 INPUT-OUTPUT SECTION.
*
 FILE-CONTROL.
     SELECT ITEMIN   ASSIGN TO AS-ITEMIN.
     SELECT PRINTOUT ASSIGN TO UT-S-ITEMLST.
*
 DATA DIVISION.
*
 FILE SECTION.
*
 FD  ITEMIN
     LABEL RECORDS ARE STANDARD
     RECORD CONTAINS 100 CHARACTERS.
*
 01  IT-RECORD.
*
     05  IT-ITEM-NUMBER       PIC X(5).
     05  IT-ITEM-DESC         PIC X(20).
     05  IT-ON-HAND           PIC S9(5)       COMP-3.
     05  FILLER               PIC X(72).
*
 FD  PRINTOUT
     LABEL RECORDS ARE STANDARD
     RECORDING MODE IS F
     RECORD CONTAINS 133 CHARACTERS
     BLOCK CONTAINS 0 RECORDS.
*
 01  PR-RECORD.
*
     05  PR-CC                PIC X.
     05  PR-ITEM-NUMBER       PIC X(5).
     05  FILLER               PIC X(3).
     05  PR-ITEM-DESC         PIC X(20).
     05  FILLER               PIC X(3).
     05  PR-ON-HAND           PIC Z(5).
     05  FILLER               PIC X(96).
*
 WORKING-STORAGE SECTION.
*
 01  SWITCHES.
*
     05  ITEM-EOF-SW          PIC X     VALUE 'N'.
         88  ITEM-EOF                   VALUE 'Y'.
```

Figure 4-3 Program listing for the entry-sequenced file-to-printer program (part 1 of 2)

```
*
 PROCEDURE DIVISION.
*
 000-PRINT-ITEM-FILE.
*
     OPEN INPUT  ITEMIN
          OUTPUT PRINTOUT.
     PERFORM 100-PRINT-ITEM-RECORD
         UNTIL ITEM-EOF.
     CLOSE ITEMIN
           PRINTOUT.
     DISPLAY 'VSELST  I  1  NORMAL EOJ'.
     STOP RUN.
*
 100-PRINT-ITEM-RECORD.
*
     PERFORM 110-READ-ITEM-RECORD.
     IF NOT ITEM-EOF
         PERFORM 120-PRINT-ITEM-LINE.
*
 110-READ-ITEM-RECORD.
*
     READ ITEMIN
         AT END
             MOVE 'Y' TO ITEM-EOF-SW.
*
 120-PRINT-ITEM-LINE.
*
     MOVE SPACE          TO PR-RECORD.
     MOVE IT-ITEM-NUMBER TO PR-ITEM-NUMBER.
     MOVE IT-ITEM-DESC   TO PR-ITEM-DESC.
     MOVE IT-ON-HAND     TO PR-ON-HAND.
     PERFORM 130-WRITE-ITEM-LINE.
*
 130-WRITE-ITEM-LINE.
*
     WRITE PR-RECORD
         AFTER ADVANCING 1 LINES.
```

Figure 4-3 Program listing for the entry-sequenced file-to-printer program (part 2 of 2)

The Procedure Division

As you can see in figure 4-1, the Procedure Division statements used to process entry-sequenced files are pretty much the same as the ones used for standard sequential files. However, there are a few variations.

The OPEN statement A new option that's available for VSAM entry-sequenced files is the EXTEND option of the OPEN statement, as in this example:

```
OPEN INPUT  ORDERS
     EXTEND INVTRANS.
```

You can use the EXTEND option when you want to add records to a file, whether during a creation or an update run. When the program opens the file, it automatically moves past the records already stored and adds the new records on to the end of the file. In other words, the entire file doesn't have to be read before the additions can be made. (This is the same as coding DISP=MOD on the DD statement for a standard sequential file.) The only I/O verb that can be used for the file when it's opened as EXTEND is the WRITE statement.

Error processing

Any program that processes a VSAM entry-sequenced file must check for error conditions indicated by the FILE STATUS field in the Procedure Division. For open and close errors, an IF statement should be coded following the OPEN or CLOSE statement just as with key-sequenced files. And each WRITE statement should be followed by an IF statement for error processing.

As you can see in figure 4-1, the AT END clause is required for all READ statements for sequential files. The AT END clause should be used for routine end-of-file processing. Since the program in figure 4-3 doesn't test for other error conditions indicated by the FILE STATUS field, serious I/O errors other than end-of-file will go undetected. Since this program doesn't modify any important data—it simply prints a report—I don't see any real need for extensive error processing here. In more critical situations, where data could be destroyed, I recommend you test the FILE STATUS field for errors, just as you would do for key-sequenced files.

IDCAMS REQUIREMENTS

Like key-sequenced files, entry-sequenced files must be defined by IDCAMS before they may be processed by a COBOL program. Figure 4-4 illustrates an IDCAMS job that defines a VSAM entry-sequenced file named H4$.EFILE on a disk volume called VSAMC1. Here, the file is allocated 20 cylinders of primary space, and the secondary allocation is 10 cylinders. As result, the file can occupy a maximum of 170 cylinders. The records are a fixed length of 80 bytes. The last parameter in the DEFINE CLUSTER statement in figure 4-4 is NONINDEXED; it is coded to indicate that the file has entry-sequenced organization.

```
//H4VS4$4   JOB   (0642,VSAMXXXXX,BD,201),
//               'DOUG LOWE'
//          EXEC   PGM=IDCAMS
//SYSPRINT  DD   SYSOUT=A
//SYSIN     DD   *
 DEFINE CLUSTER -
        (NAME(H4$.EFILE) -
          VOLUMES(VSAMC1) -
          CYLINDERS(20 10) -
          RECORDSIZE(80 80) -
          NONINDEXED )
/*
```

Figure 4-4 Defining an entry-sequenced file with IDCAMS

The other IDCAMS functions described in chapter 3 operate the same for entry-sequenced files as they do for key-sequenced files. One minor variation you may notice is that the output from a PRINT statement is somewhat different. Instead of labeling each record with its record key value, the entry-sequenced records are labeled with their RBA values. *RBA*, or *Relative-Byte-Address*, indicates each record's displacement in bytes from the beginning of the file. If, for example, the records are 80 bytes long, the RBA of the first record is 0, because it is at the very beginning of the file. Then, the RBA of the second record is 80, the third 160, and so on.

JCL REQUIREMENTS

The JCL required to execute a program that processes an entry-sequenced file is exactly the same as that required for key-sequenced files. The DD statement for the entry-sequenced file requires only two parameters: DSNAME and DISP. DISP is always coded OLD.

DISCUSSION

One question you may be asking right now is this: Why aren't I covering VSAM entry-sequenced files in more detail? This is a legitimate question. The answer is that VSAM entry-sequenced files are seldom, if ever, used. For one thing, VSAM provides no substantial improvement over the other sequential access methods in terms of efficiency. Second, and even more important, VSAM entry-sequenced file processing is more limited than non-VSAM sequential file processing. For example, VSAM provides no automatic handling of generation data sets—a must for many sequential applications. Perhaps IBM will someday correct these problems. Until then, entry-sequenced VSAM files will rarely be used.

Terminology

RBA

Relative Byte Address

Objectives

1. Given a programming problem involving the use of a VSAM entry-sequenced file, code an acceptable COBOL solution.

Problems

1. Figure 2-10 is a VSAM indexed-file load program. Code the necessary changes to this program so that the file being loaded is an entry-sequenced file rather than a key-sequenced file. Assume that the file may or may not already have records in it; if there are records in the file, the new records should be added to the end. Also change the error processing so that if any type of read error is encountered, the program displays a message indicating the item number and FILE STATUS value and terminates via the ABEND100 subprogram introduced in chapter 2.

Solutions

1. Figure 4-5 shows the changes required. Here, three changes have been made. First, the SELECT statement has been changed so that it defines an entry-sequenced file. Second, the EXTEND option has been included in the OPEN statement so that any existing records in the file will be bypassed. And third, the IF statement following the WRITE statement has been changed so that it displays a message and terminates the program.

```
 IDENTIFICATION DIVISION.
*
 PROGRAM-ID.  VSECR.
*
 ENVIRONMENT DIVISION.
*
 INPUT-OUTPUT SECTION.
*
 FILE-CONTROL.
     SELECT INVCARDS ASSIGN TO UT-S-INVCARDS.
     SELECT INVMSTR  ASSIGN TO AS-INVMSTR
                     ORGANIZATION IS SEQUENTIAL
                     ACCESS IS SEQUENTIAL
                     FILE STATUS IS INVMSTR-ERROR-CODE.
     .
     .
 DATA DIVISION.
     .
     .
 PROCEDURE DIVISION.
*
 000-CREATE-INVENTORY-FILE.
*
     OPEN INPUT  INVCARDS
          EXTEND INVMSTR.
     .
     .
 120-WRITE-INVENTORY-RECORD.
*
     WRITE IM-RECORD.
     IF INVMSTR-ERROR-CODE NOT = 00
         DISPLAY 'VSECR  A  2  WRITE ERROR FOR INVMSTR. ITEM NO '
                 IM-ITEM-NUMBER
                 '.  FILE STATUS '
                 INVMSTR-ERROR-CODE '.'
         CALL 'ABEND100'.
```

Figure 4-5 Modifications to the key-sequenced load program

5

Processing Relative-Record Files

This chapter shows you how to process a VSAM relative-record data set (RRDS). A relative file may be processed either sequentially or randomly by specifying each record's position in the file. In other words, each record is numbered. The first record in the file is record number one, the next record is number two, and so on.

Figure 5-1 illustrates a VSAM relative-record file. The file consists of *record slots* that contain either data or free space. Notice that it is actually the record slot—*not* the data record—that is numbered. When a relative file is processed sequentially, the data records are accessed in sequential order. Any empty slots are automatically skipped during sequential processing. When random processing is used, it is the slots that are accessed. Thus, in figure 5-1, it is possible to access slot 9 using random processing, even though no data is stored there.

Additions to a relative file are handled in one of two ways. First, records may be added sequentially to the end of the file, just as they are for entry-sequenced files. Second, a record may be inserted into an empty slot within the file. To do this, the program must be able to determine which slots in the file are empty.

When a relative-record file contains variable-length records, the record slots are as long as the longest record in the file. Thus, any record may be expanded to its maximum length without affecting the

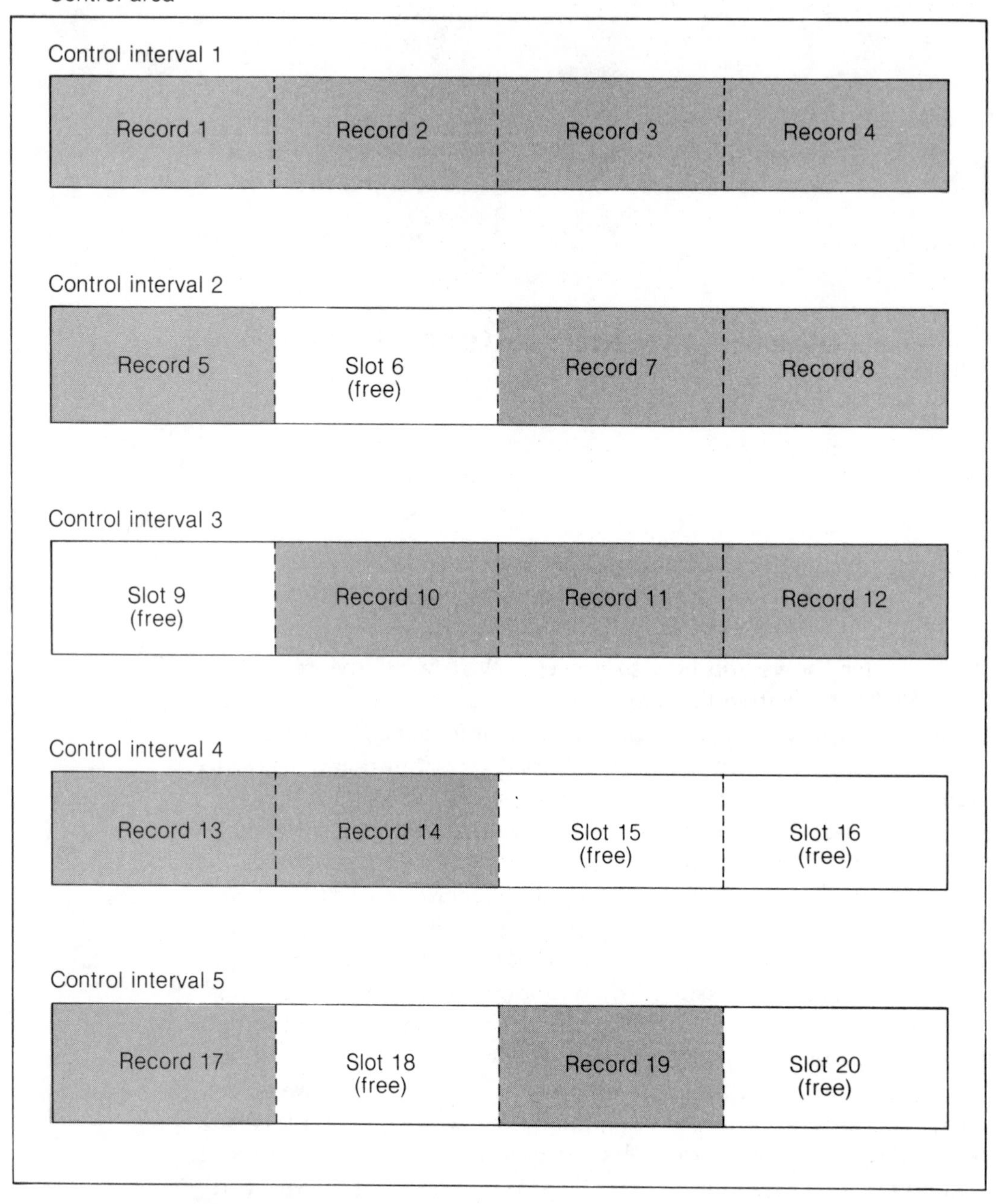

Figure 5-1 A VSAM relative-record data set

other records in the control interval. Of course, this also means that most of the slots will contain unused space.

In order to develop COBOL programs that process relative-record files, you must know three things. First, you must know the COBOL elements that are used to process VSAM relative files. Second, you must know how to define, copy, and print relative files using IDCAMS. And third, you must know how to code the JCL statements necessary to execute a COBOL program that processes a relative file.

COBOL REQUIREMENTS

Like key-sequenced files, relative-record files may be processed either sequentially or randomly. When sequential processing is used, the records are automatically accessed in sequential order. When random processing is used, you must specify the number of each record you wish to process.

Figure 5-2 summarizes the elements used for processing VSAM relative-record files using sequential or random access. With just a few exceptions, these elements are identical to the ones used for key-sequenced files.

The Environment Division

The format for the assignment-name used in the ASSIGN clause of the SELECT statement for a VSAM relative file is this:

```
comment-ddname
```

As you can see, this is the same format as the one used for key-sequenced files. In the sample programs in this topic, I have omitted the comment so the assignment-name is simply the ddname specified in the JCL.

You must specify ORGANIZATION IS RELATIVE in the SELECT statement for a VSAM relative file (for a non-VSAM relative file, the organization is specified in the ASSIGN clause). Then, you use the ACCESS MODE clause to specify whether the file will be processed sequentially or randomly.

The RELATIVE KEY clause specifies a field that will be used to indicate the relative position of each record in the file. Unlike the RECORD KEY field for keyed files, which is defined in the File Section, the RELATIVE KEY field is defined in the Working Storage Section. When sequential processing is used, the RELATIVE KEY clause needs to be specified only if the START statement is used. The RELATIVE KEY field operates like the NOMINAL KEY field does for non-VSAM relative files.

The FILE STATUS clause operates just as it does for other types of VSAM files. Whenever an I/O statement is executed, a code is placed in the FILE STATUS field to indicate whether the statement executed properly or an error occured. The FILE STATUS codes most frequently encountered for VSAM relative-record files are shown in figure 5-3.

```
IDENTIFICATION DIVISION.
     .
     .
ENVIRONMENT DIVISION.
     .
     .
INPUT-OUTPUT SECTION.
FILE-CONTROL.
    SELECT file-name ASSIGN TO assignment-name
                     ORGANIZATION IS RELATIVE

                     ACCESS MODE IS {SEQUENTIAL}
                                    {RANDOM    }

                     RELATIVE KEY IS data-name
                     FILE STATUS IS data-name.
     .
     .
DATA DIVISION.
FILE SECTION.
FD  file-name
    LABEL RECORDS ARE STANDARD
    RECORD CONTAINS integer CHARACTERS
    [BLOCK CONTAINS integer RECORDS].
     .
WORKING-STORAGE SECTION.
     .
     .
```

Note: The RELATIVE KEY field and the FILE STATUS field must be defined in the Working-Storage Section.

Figure 5-2 COBOL elements for processing relative-record files (part 1 of 2)

The Data Division

Coding in the Data Division for relative-record files is the same as it is for key-sequenced files, except that the key field specified in the SELECT statement is defined in the Working-Storage Section instead of the File Section. The LABEL RECORDS clause is always required but treated as comments, the RECORDING MODE clause is invalid, and the BLOCK CONTAINS clause is optional and usually omitted.

The Procedure Division

If you compare the Procedure Division elements in figure 5-2 with those in figures 2-6 and 2-14, you will see that they are identical. The same I-O statements are used for key-sequenced and relative-record files.

One other point that should be mentioned is that when a record is deleted by the DELETE statement, the space occupied by that record is released—but the record's position in the file is still there. In

```
PROCEDURE DIVISION.
    .
    .
          ⎧INPUT   file-name ...⎫
    OPEN  ⎨OUTPUT  file-name ...⎬  ...
          ⎩I-O     file-name ...⎭

    CLOSE file-name ...
```

Sequential access

```
                                ⎧EQUAL TO        ⎫
                                ⎪=               ⎪
    START file-name [KEY IS     ⎨GREATER THAN    ⎬  data-name].
                                ⎪>               ⎪
                                ⎪NOT LESS THAN   ⎪
                                ⎩NOT <           ⎭

    READ file-name RECORD
        [INTO data-name]
        [AT END imperative-statement].

    WRITE record-name
        [FROM data-name]
        [INVALID KEY imperative-statement].

    REWRITE record-name
        [FROM data-name]
        [INVALID KEY imperative-statement].

    DELETE file-name RECORD.
```

Random access

```
    READ file-name RECORD
        [INTO data-name]
        [INVALID KEY imperative-statement].

    WRITE record-name
        [FROM data-name]
        [INVALID KEY imperative-statement].

    REWRITE record-name
        [FROM data-name]
        [INVALID KEY imperative-statement].

    DELETE file-name RECORD
        [INVALID KEY imperative-statement].
```

Figure 5-2 COBOL elements for processing relative-record files (part 2 of 2)

other words, if you delete record 17, an empty position will be left in the file. Using random access, this empty position may be filled with new data. When reading the file sequentially, empty record positions are ignored. For example, suppose again that record 17 has been deleted. After you read record 16 using sequential access, the next READ statement will read record 18—the deleted record is skipped.

FILE STATUS

Value	Meaning
00	Successful completion
10	End of file
22	Record already exists
23	Record not found

Figure 5-3 Common FILE STATUS values for relative files

Sequential processing

Figures 5-4 and 5-5 present the structure chart and program listing for a simple file-to-printer program that illustrates sequential processing of a relative file. The records are 32 bytes long and contain these fields: item number (5 bytes), item description (20 bytes), on-hand balance (a 5-digit COMP-3 field that requires 3 bytes of storage), and four FILLER bytes. When the original relative file was created, the record numbers (relative keys) were calculated by subtracting 1000 from the item number in each record (there are no records with an item number less than 1001). In other words, the file was loaded on a random basis so it will contain empty slots unless the item numbers were numbered consecutively.

As you can see in the structure chart in figure 5-4, the main processing module, module 200, reads an input record and writes it on the report. Before module 200 is executed, however, module 100 is called to read an input card that supplies the value of the first item number to be processed. You can see in figure 5-5 (the complete program listing) that module 100 subtracts 1000 from this value to determine the proper record number, and a START statement is used in module 000 to tell the program to begin processing at the specified record. If the starting value is invalid (not a positive integer), an error message is displayed and INVMSTR-EOF-SW is set to Y so the program skips module 200 and ends.

Since the records are read sequentially, it is not necessary for module 200 to maintain the proper record number in the RELATIVE KEY field. In fact, if the START statement weren't used in this program, the RELATIVE KEY clause could be omitted from the SELECT statement for the relative file.

You may have noticed in figure 5-5 that I used the AT END clause for the READ statement in module 210. As a result, any serious I/O error (other than end-of-file) will go undetected by this program. However, since this program doesn't modify any important

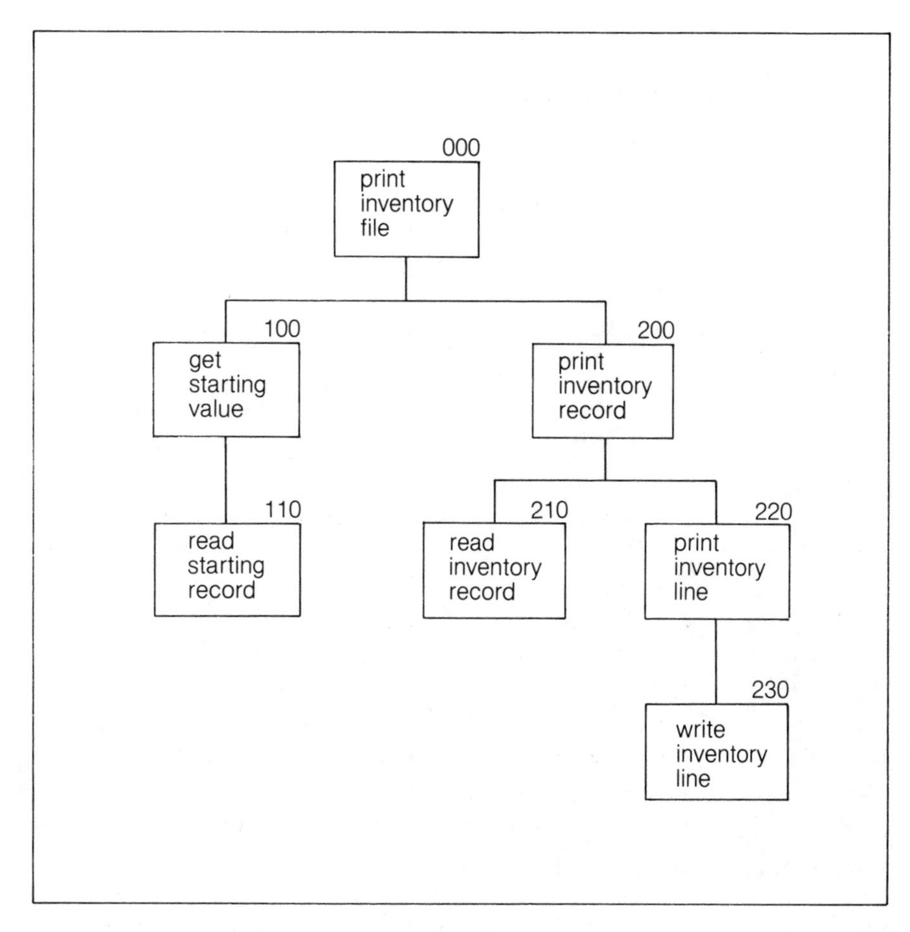

Figure 5-4 Structure chart for a relative-record file-to-printer program

data—it simply prints a report—I don't see any real need for extensive error processing. In more critical situations, where live data could be destroyed, I recommend you test the FILE STATUS field for errors, just as you would do for a key-sequenced file.

Random processing

Figure 5-6 shows a structure chart for a program that does a random update of a relative file. The complete listing for this program is given in figure 5-7. Since the COBOL elements used to process relative files are nearly identical to the elements used for key-sequenced files, this program is almost identical to the key-sequenced file update program presented in figure 2-15.

In the Environment Division, the only difference is that the SELECT statement specifies RELATIVE organization and a RELATIVE KEY. As for the Procedure Division, it should be easy enough to follow. The main processing module, module 100, first

```
 IDENTIFICATION DIVISION.
*
 PROGRAM-ID.  VSRLST.
*
 ENVIRONMENT DIVISION.
*
 INPUT-OUTPUT SECTION.
*
 FILE-CONTROL.
     SELECT ITEMSTRT ASSIGN TO UT-S-ITEMSTRT.
     SELECT INVMSTR  ASSIGN TO INVMSTR
                     ORGANIZATION IS RELATIVE
                     ACCESS IS SEQUENTIAL
                     RELATIVE KEY IS IM-STARTING-VALUE.
     SELECT ITEMLST  ASSIGN TO UT-S-ITEMLST.
*
 DATA DIVISION.
*
 FILE SECTION.
*
 FD  ITEMSTRT
     LABEL RECORDS ARE STANDARD
     RECORDING MODE IS F
     RECORD CONTAINS 80 CHARACTERS
     BLOCK CONTAINS 0 RECORDS.
*
 01  IS-AREA             PIC X(80).
*
 FD  INVMSTR
     LABEL RECORDS ARE STANDARD
     RECORD CONTAINS 32 CHARACTERS.
*
 01  IM-AREA             PIC X(32).
*
 FD  ITEMLST
     LABEL RECORDS ARE STANDARD
     RECORDING MODE IS F
     RECORD CONTAINS 133 CHARACTERS
     BLOCK CONTAINS 0 RECORDS.
*
 01  PRINT-AREA                  PIC X(133).
*
 WORKING-STORAGE SECTION.
*
 01  SWITCHES.
*
     05  INVMSTR-EOF-SW      PIC X     VALUE 'N'.
         88  INVMSTR-EOF               VALUE 'Y'.
     05  ITEMSTRT-EOF-SW     PIC X     VALUE 'N'.
         88  ITEMSTRT-EOF              VALUE 'Y'.
*
 01  RELATIVE-KEY-FIELD.
```

Figure 5-5 Program listing for a relative-record file-to-printer program (part 1 of 3)

```
*
     05   IM-STARTING-VALUE    PIC 9(5).
*
 01  IM-RECORD.
*
     05   IM-ITEM-NUMBER       PIC X(5).
     05   IM-ITEM-DESC         PIC X(20).
     05   IM-ON-HAND           PIC S9(5)        COMP-3.
     05   FILLER               PIC X(72).
*
 01  IS-RECORD.
*
     05   IS-STARTING-ITEM-NUMBER      PIC 9(5).
     05   FILLER                       PIC X(75).
*
 01  REPORT-LINE.
*
     05   RL-CC                PIC X.
     05   RL-ITEM-NUMBER       PIC X(5).
     05   FILLER               PIC X(5)    VALUE SPACE.
     05   RL-ITEM-DESC         PIC X(20).
     05   FILLER               PIC X(3)    VALUE SPACE.
     05   RL-ON-HAND           PIC ZZZZ9.
     05   FILLER               PIC X(94)   VALUE SPACE.
*
 PROCEDURE DIVISION.
*
 000-PRINT-INVENTORY-FILE.
*
     OPEN INPUT  ITEMSTRT
                 INVMSTR
          OUTPUT ITEMLST.
     PERFORM 100-GET-STARTING-VALUE.
     START INVMSTR
         KEY IS NOT LESS THAN IM-STARTING-VALUE
         INVALID KEY
             DISPLAY 'VSRLST  A  2  INVALID VALUE FOR '
                     'STARTING KEY ' IS-STARTING-ITEM-NUMBER
             MOVE 'Y' TO INVMSTR-EOF-SW.
     PERFORM 200-PRINT-INVENTORY-RECORD
         UNTIL INVMSTR-EOF.
     CLOSE ITEMSTRT
           INVMSTR
           ITEMLST.
     DISPLAY 'VSRLST  I  1  NORMAL EOJ'.
     STOP RUN.
*
 100-GET-STARTING-VALUE.
*
     PERFORM 110-READ-STARTING-RECORD.
     SUBTRACT 1000 FROM IS-STARTING-ITEM-NUMBER
         GIVING IM-STARTING-VALUE.
```

Figure 5-5 Program listing for a relative-record file-to-printer program (part 2 of 3)

```
*
 110-READ-STARTING-RECORD.
*
     READ ITEMSTRT
         AT END
             MOVE 'Y' TO ITEMSTRT-EOF-SW
             MOVE 1001 TO IS-STARTING-ITEM-NUMBER.
*
 200-PRINT-INVENTORY-RECORD.
*
     PERFORM 210-READ-INVENTORY-RECORD.
     IF NOT INVMSTR-EOF
         PERFORM 220-PRINT-INVENTORY-LINE.
*
 210-READ-INVENTORY-RECORD.
*
     READ INVMSTR INTO IM-RECORD
         AT END
             MOVE 'Y' TO INVMSTR-EOF-SW.
*
 220-PRINT-INVENTORY-LINE.
*
     MOVE IM-ITEM-NUMBER TO RL-ITEM-NUMBER.
     MOVE IM-ITEM-DESC   TO RL-ITEM-DESC.
     MOVE IM-ON-HAND     TO RL-ON-HAND.
     MOVE REPORT-LINE    TO PRINT-AREA.
     PERFORM 230-WRITE-INVENTORY-LINE.
*
 230-WRITE-INVENTORY-LINE.
*
     WRITE PRINT-AREA
         AFTER ADVANCING 1 LINES.
```

Figure 5-5 Program listing for a relative-record file-to-printer program (part 3 of 3)

reads a transaction record, calculates the RELATIVE KEY field by subtracting 1000 from the item number, and sets MASTER-FOUND-SW to Y. Then, the master file is read in module 120. If the FILE STATUS field is 23 after the master file is read, it indicates that no data has been stored in that record position—in other words, there is no master record for that item. So N is moved to MASTER-FOUND-SW, and the transaction is written on the error file. If the FILE STATUS indicates a serious error condition, the program is terminated. If the master is found, it is changed and rewritten, and the transaction is recorded on the update listing.

So you could focus on the elements required for relative files, I did not code all of the error handling routines that a production program should include. In actual practice, however, you should consider checking the FILE STATUS field after every I/O statement. If

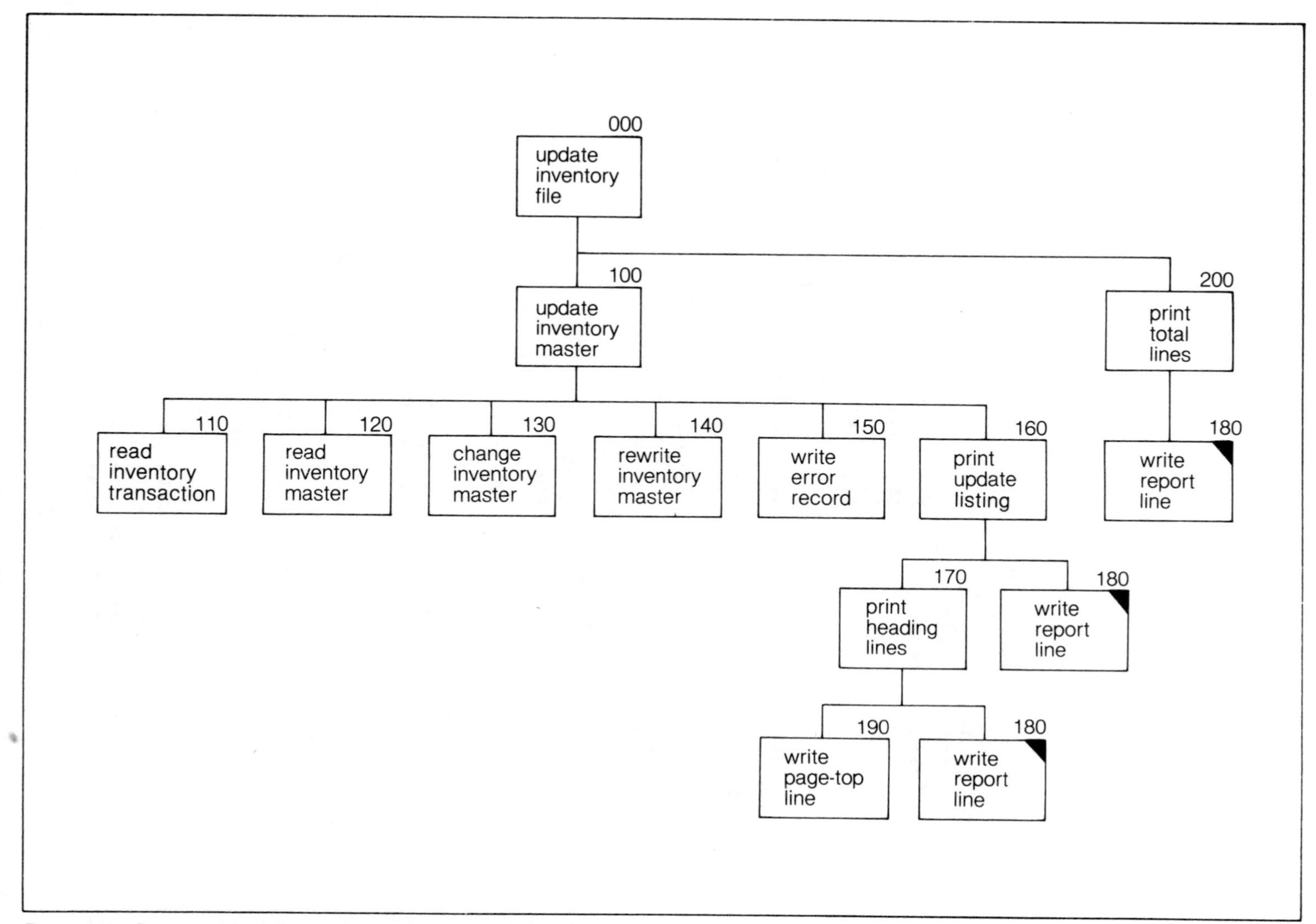

Figure 5-6 Structure chart for a relative-record file-update program

```
IDENTIFICATION DIVISION.
*
PROGRAM-ID.  VSRRUPD.
*
ENVIRONMENT DIVISION.
*
CONFIGURATION SECTION.
*
SPECIAL-NAMES.
    C01 IS PAGE-TOP.
*
INPUT-OUTPUT SECTION.
*
FILE-CONTROL.
    SELECT TRANFILE ASSIGN TO UT-S-TRANFILE.
    SELECT INVMSTR  ASSIGN TO INVMSTR
                    ORGANIZATION IS RELATIVE
                    ACCESS IS RANDOM
                    RELATIVE KEY IS MA-RECORD-NUMBER
                    FILE STATUS IS INVMSTR-ERROR-CODE.
    SELECT ERRFILE  ASSIGN TO UT-S-ERRFILE.
    SELECT UPDLIST  ASSIGN TO UT-S-UPDLIST.
*
DATA DIVISION.
*
FILE SECTION.
*
FD  TRANFILE
    LABEL RECORDS ARE STANDARD
    RECORDING MODE IS F
    RECORD CONTAINS 24 CHARACTERS
    BLOCK CONTAINS 0 RECORDS.
*
01  TR-AREA                  PIC X(24).
*
FD  INVMSTR
    LABEL RECORDS ARE STANDARD
    RECORD CONTAINS 32 CHARACTERS.
*
01  IM-RECORD.
*
    05  IM-ITEM-NUMBER       PIC X(5).
    05  IM-ITEM-DESC         PIC X(20).
    05  IM-ON-HAND           PIC S9(5)       COMP-3.
    05  FILLER               PIC X(4).
*
FD  ERRFILE
    LABEL RECORDS ARE STANDARD
    RECORDING MODE IS F
    RECORD CONTAINS 24 CHARACTERS
    BLOCK CONTAINS 0 RECORDS.
```

Figure 5-7 Program listing for a relative-record file-update program (part 1 of 6)

```
*
 01   ER-RECORD               PIC X(24).
*
 FD   UPDLIST
      LABEL RECORDS ARE OMITTED
      RECORDING MODE IS F
      RECORD CONTAINS 133 CHARACTERS
      BLOCK CONTAINS 0 RECORDS.
*
 01   PRINT-AREA              PIC X(133).
*
 WORKING-STORAGE SECTION.
*
 01   SWITCHES.
*
      05   TRAN-EOF-SW                       PIC X     VALUE 'N'.
           88   TRAN-EOF                               VALUE 'Y'.
      05   MASTER-FOUND-SW                   PIC X     VALUE 'N'.
           88   MASTER-FOUND                           VALUE 'Y'.
*
 01   RELATIVE-KEY-FIELD.
*
      05   MA-RECORD-NUMBER                  PIC 9(5).
*
 01   FILE-STATUS-FIELD.
*
      05   INVMSTR-ERROR-CODE      PIC XX.
*
 01   COUNT-FIELDS                 COMP-3.
*
      05   TRANS-PROCESSED-COUNT   PIC S9(5)      VALUE ZERO.
      05   UNMATCHED-TRANS-COUNT   PIC S9(5)      VALUE ZERO.
*
 01   PRINT-FIELDS                 COMP           SYNC.
*
      05   LINE-COUNT              PIC S99        VALUE +99.
      05   LINES-ON-PAGE           PIC S99        VALUE +57.
      05   SPACE-CONTROL           PIC S9.
*
 01   TR-RECORD.
*
      05   TR-ITEM-NUMBER          PIC 9(5).
      05   TR-VENDOR-NUMBER        PIC X(5).
      05   TR-RECEIPT-DATE         PIC X(6).
      05   TR-RECEIPT-QUANTITY     PIC S9(5)      COMP-3.
      05   FILLER                  PIC X(5).
*
 01   HDG-LINE-1.
*
      05   HDG1-CC            PIC X.
      05   FILLER             PIC X(1)     VALUE SPACE.
```

Figure 5-7 Program listing for a relative-record file-update program (part 2 of 6)

```
           05   FILLER              PIC X(4)     VALUE 'ITEM'.
           05   FILLER              PIC X(2)     VALUE SPACE.
           05   FILLER              PIC X(6)     VALUE 'VENDOR'.
           05   FILLER              PIC X(4)     VALUE SPACE.
           05   FILLER              PIC X(7)     VALUE 'RECEIPT'.
           05   FILLER              PIC X(2)     VALUE SPACE.
           05   FILLER              PIC X(7)     VALUE 'RECEIPT'.
           05   FILLER              PIC X(99)    VALUE SPACE.
      *
       01  HDG-LINE-2.
      *
           05   HDG2-CC             PIC X.
           05   FILLER              PIC X(2)     VALUE SPACE.
           05   FILLER              PIC X(3)     VALUE 'NO.'.
           05   FILLER              PIC X(4)     VALUE SPACE.
           05   FILLER              PIC X(3)     VALUE 'NO.'.
           05   FILLER              PIC X(6)     VALUE SPACE.
           05   FILLER              PIC X(4)     VALUE 'DATE'.
           05   FILLER              PIC X(4)     VALUE SPACE.
           05   FILLER              PIC X(6)     VALUE 'AMOUNT'.
           05   FILLER              PIC X(100)   VALUE SPACE.
      *
       01  NEXT-REPORT-LINE.
      *
           05   NRL-CC                        PIC X.
           05   NRL-ITEM-NUMBER               PIC X(5).
           05   FILLER                        PIC X(3)     VALUE SPACE.
           05   NRL-VENDOR-NUMBER             PIC Z(5).
           05   FILLER                        PIC X(3)     VALUE SPACE.
           05   NRL-RECEIPT-DATE              PIC 99B99B99.
           05   FILLER                        PIC X(3)     VALUE SPACE.
           05   NRL-RECEIPT-QUANTITY          PIC ZZZZ9.
           05   FILLER                        PIC X(100)   VALUE SPACE.
      *
       01  TOTAL-LINE-1.
      *
           05   TL1-CC                        PIC X.
           05   TL1-TRANS-PROCESSED           PIC ZZ,ZZ9.
           05   FILLER                        PIC X(23)
                                              VALUE ' TRANSACTIONS PROCESSED'.
           05   FILLER                        PIC X(103)   VALUE SPACE.
      *
       01  TOTAL-LINE-2.
      *
           05   TL2-CC                        PIC X.
           05   TL2-UNMATCHED-TRANS           PIC ZZ,ZZ9.
           05   FILLER                        PIC X(23)
                                              VALUE ' UNMATCHED TRANSACTIONS'.
           05   FILLER                        PIC X(103)   VALUE SPACE.
```

Figure 5-7 Program listing for a relative-record file-update program (part 3 of 6)

```
 PROCEDURE DIVISION.
*
 000-UPDATE-INVENTORY-FILE.
*
     OPEN INPUT  TRANFILE
          I-O    INVMSTR
          OUTPUT ERRFILE
                 UPDLIST.
     PERFORM 100-UPDATE-INVENTORY-MASTER
         UNTIL TRAN-EOF.
     PERFORM 200-PRINT-TOTAL-LINES.
     CLOSE TRANFILE
           INVMSTR
           ERRFILE
           UPDLIST.
     DISPLAY 'VSRRUPD  I  1  NORMAL EOJ'.
     STOP RUN.
*
 100-UPDATE-INVENTORY-MASTER.
*
     PERFORM 110-READ-INVENTORY-TRANSACTION.
     IF NOT TRAN-EOF
         SUBTRACT 1000 FROM TR-ITEM-NUMBER
             GIVING MA-RECORD-NUMBER
         MOVE 'Y' TO MASTER-FOUND-SW
         PERFORM 120-READ-INVENTORY-MASTER
         IF MASTER-FOUND
             PERFORM 130-CHANGE-INVENTORY-MASTER
             PERFORM 140-REWRITE-INVENTORY-MASTER
             PERFORM 160-PRINT-UPDATE-LISTING
         ELSE
             PERFORM 150-WRITE-ERROR-RECORD.
*
 110-READ-INVENTORY-TRANSACTION.
*
     READ TRANFILE INTO TR-RECORD
         AT END
             MOVE 'Y' TO TRAN-EOF-SW.
     IF NOT TRAN-EOF
         ADD 1 TO TRANS-PROCESSED-COUNT.
*
 120-READ-INVENTORY-MASTER.
*
     READ INVMSTR.
     IF INVMSTR-ERROR-CODE NOT = 00
         IF INVMSTR-ERROR-CODE = 23
             MOVE 'N' TO MASTER-FOUND-SW
         ELSE
             DISPLAY 'VSRRUPD  A  2  READ ERROR FOR INVMSTR.  '
                     'ITEM NO. ' MA-RECORD-NUMBER
                     '.  FILE STATUS '  INVMSTR-ERROR-CODE '.'
```

Figure 5-7 Program listing for a relative-record file-update program (part 4 of 6)

```
MOVE 'N' TO MASTER-FOUND-SW
MOVE 'Y' TO TRAN-EOF-SW.
*
 130-CHANGE-INVENTORY-MASTER.
*
     ADD TR-RECEIPT-QUANTITY TO IM-ON-HAND.
*
 140-REWRITE-INVENTORY-MASTER.
*
     REWRITE IM-RECORD.
     IF INVMSTR-ERROR-CODE NOT = 00
         DISPLAY 'VSRRUPD  A  3  REWRITE ERROR FOR INVMSTR.  '
                 'ITEM NO. ' MA-RECORD-NUMBER
                 '.  FILE STATUS ' INVMSTR-ERROR-CODE '.'
         MOVE 'Y' TO TRAN-EOF-SW.
*
 150-WRITE-ERROR-RECORD.
*
     WRITE ER-RECORD FROM TR-RECORD.
     ADD 1 TO UNMATCHED-TRANS-COUNT.
*
 160-PRINT-UPDATE-LISTING.
*
     IF LINE-COUNT GREATER THAN LINES-ON-PAGE
         PERFORM 170-PRINT-HEADING-LINES.
     MOVE TR-ITEM-NUMBER        TO NRL-ITEM-NUMBER.
     MOVE TR-VENDOR-NUMBER      TO NRL-VENDOR-NUMBER.
     MOVE TR-RECEIPT-DATE       TO NRL-RECEIPT-DATE.
     MOVE TR-RECEIPT-QUANTITY   TO NRL-RECEIPT-QUANTITY.
     MOVE NEXT-REPORT-LINE      TO PRINT-AREA.
     PERFORM 180-WRITE-REPORT-LINE.
     MOVE 1 TO SPACE-CONTROL.
*
 170-PRINT-HEADING-LINES.
*
     MOVE HDG-LINE-1 TO PRINT-AREA.
     PERFORM 190-WRITE-PAGE-TOP-LINE.
     MOVE HDG-LINE-2 TO PRINT-AREA.
     MOVE 1 TO SPACE-CONTROL.
     PERFORM 180-WRITE-REPORT-LINE.
     MOVE 2 TO SPACE-CONTROL.
*
 180-WRITE-REPORT-LINE.
*
     WRITE PRINT-AREA
         AFTER ADVANCING SPACE-CONTROL LINES.
     ADD SPACE-CONTROL TO LINE-COUNT.
```

Figure 5-7 Program listing for a relative-record file-update program (part 5 of 6)

```
*
 190-WRITE-PAGE-TOP-LINE.
*
     WRITE PRINT-AREA
         AFTER ADVANCING PAGE-TOP.
     MOVE ZERO TO LINE-COUNT.
*
 200-PRINT-TOTAL-LINES.
*
     MOVE TRANS-PROCESSED-COUNT TO TL1-TRANS-PROCESSED.
     MOVE TOTAL-LINE-1 TO PRINT-AREA.
     MOVE 3 TO SPACE-CONTROL.
     PERFORM 180-WRITE-REPORT-LINE.
     MOVE UNMATCHED-TRANS-COUNT TO TL2-UNMATCHED-TRANS.
     MOVE TOTAL-LINE-2 TO PRINT-AREA.
     MOVE 1 TO SPACE-CONTROL.
     PERFORM 180-WRITE-REPORT-LINE.
```

Figure 5-7 Program listing for a relative-record file-update program (part 6 of 6)

an I/O error could lead to a serious problem, your program should print an appropriate message and call a subprogram for abnormal program termination. You code these routines just as you would for a key-sequenced file.

IDCAMS REQUIREMENTS

Like key-sequenced files, relative-record files must be defined by IDCAMS before they may be processed by a COBOL program. The DEFINE CLUSTER statement is used for this purpose. Figure 5-8 illustrates an IDCAMS job that defines a VSAM relative-record file named H4$.RFILE on a disk volume called VSAMC1. Here, the file is allocated 100 tracks of primary space, and the secondary allocation is 50 tracks. As a result, the file will occupy a maximum of 850 tracks (100 + 50 x 15 = 850). The records are a fixed length of 50 bytes. The last parameter in the DEFINE CLUSTER statement is NUMBERED; it is coded to indicate that the file has relative-record organization.

The other IDCAMS functions described in chapter 3 operate the same for relative-record files as they do for key-sequenced files. One minor variation you may notice is that the output from a PRINT statement is somewhat different. Instead of labeling each record with its record key value, the relative records are labeled with their relative-record numbers.

```
//H4VS5$8  JOB   (0642,VSAMXXXXX,BD,201),
//               'DOUG LOWE'
//         EXEC   PGM=IDCAMS
//SYSPRINT DD   SYSOUT=A
//SYSIN    DD   *
 DEFINE CLUSTER -
          (NAME(H4$.RFILE) -
            VOLUMES(VSAMC1) -
            TRACKS(100 50) -
            RECORDSIZE(50 50) -
            NUMBERED )
/*
```

Figure 5-8 Defining a relative-record file with IDCAMS

JCL REQUIREMENTS

The JCL required to execute a program that processes a relative-record file is exactly the same as that required for key-sequenced files. The DD statement for the relative file requires only two parameters: DSNAME and DISP. DISP is always coded as OLD.

DISCUSSION

I hope you now appreciate the similarities in the COBOL for relative-record and key-sequenced processing. There are only two differences: the ORGANIZATION clause specifies RELATIVE instead of INDEXED, and the RELATIVE KEY clause is used instead of the RECORD KEY clause.

Quite frankly, there are few applications that are well suited for relative files. In most cases, it is difficult to convert a record key to a unique relative record number, so indexed files are used instead. However, in those cases where it is easy to generate unique record numbers, relative-record files can be processed much more efficiently than indexed files because of a simplified index structure (relative record files only maintain the lowest level index which points to the control interval containing the record).

Objectives

1. Given a problem involving VSAM relative-record files, code a COBOL solution.

PART FOUR

VSAM in a DOS/VS Environment

Throughout this book, I have assumed you are using VSAM on an OS/VS system. However, VSAM is also available on DOS/VS systems. This part presents the variations you will encounter on a DOS system.

6

DOS Variations

This chapter presents the significant variations you will encounter if you are using VSAM on a DOS system. There are two major versions of DOS that support VSAM: DOS/VS and DOS/VSE. DOS/VS is simply a virtual storage version of standard DOS. DOS/VSE is an extended version of DOS/VS that allows up to twelve partitions for multiprogramming as well as several other enhancements. In most cases, VSAM is the same whether you are using DOS/VS or DOS/VSE.

All of the examples presented in this chapter are for release 2 of DOS/VSE. This release simplifies the JCL requirements for VSAM processing by taking advantage of more of the information stored in the VSAM catalog. Any additional requirements for earlier versions of DOS/VSE and for DOS/VS will be explained but not illustrated.

In general, there are three areas of variation for DOS VSAM: (1) the COBOL language elements used for processing VSAM files, (2) the JCL requirements for VSAM files, and (3) IDCAMS control statement variations. This chapter covers all three areas.

COBOL VARIATIONS

The DOS COBOL elements used to process VSAM indexed and relative files are exactly the same as the OS elements with one exception: the assignment name in the ASSIGN clause of the SELECT statement. Under DOS, the assignment name follows this format for key-sequenced and relative-record files:

```
SYSnnn [-class] [-device] [-name]
```

Although this is similar to the assignment name for other types of DOS files, note that the class and device entries are optional for VSAM files. They are treated as documentation. Usually, only the SYSnnn and name fields are coded, like this:

```
SYS020-INVMSTR
```

The DOS COBOL elements for entry-sequenced files are the same as the elements presented in chapter 4 except for the assignment name. For entry-sequenced files, the DOS format is this:

```
SYSnnn [-class] [-device] -AS [-name]
```

Again, the class and device entries are usually omitted, so the assignment name is coded like this example:

```
SYS024-AS-INVTRAN
```

One other variation you will encounter when writing DOS COBOL programs for VSAM files is the use of assembler-language subprograms to cause abnormal program termination. DOS provides two assembler macro instructions to cause program termination: CANCEL and DUMP. Figure 6-1 shows two assembler-language subprograms built around these macros. The first one, CANCEL, uses the CANCEL macro to cause the program to be terminated without producing a storage dump. The second one, DUMP, causes a storage

Abend without dump

```
CANCEL      START  0
            SAVE   (14,12)
            CANCEL
            END
```

Abend with dump

```
DUMP        START  0
            SAVE   (14,12)
            DUMP
            END
```

Figure 6-1 DOS assembler subprograms for terminating a COBOL program

```
// DLBL   file-name,'file-id',,VSAM

// EXEC   program-name,SIZE= {nK  }
                              {AUTO}
```

Figure 6-2 DOS JCL required for a VSAM file

dump to be printed as the program is terminated. These subprograms are used the same as the ABEND100 and ABEND200 subprograms for OS; the only difference is the name of the subprogram specified in the CALL statement. Thus, to cause a program to be terminated and a dump printed under DOS, you would code a CALL statement like this:

```
CALL 'DUMP'.
```

DOS JCL FOR VSAM FILES

Under DOS, like OS, most of the file specifications are given when a cluster is defined. As a result, the JCL for running a COBOL program that uses a VSAM file is minimal. For creation (load) programs as well as other processing programs, the JCL for a VSAM file follows the pattern shown in figure 6-2.

To define the VSAM file, a DLBL statement is used. As you can see in figure 6-2, only three parameters are required on the DLBL statement: file-name, file-id, and VSAM. You are already familiar with the first two parameters; the third parameter simply indicates to DOS that the file being processed is a VSAM file.

In the EXEC statement, the SIZE parameter is always required. It specifies how many K bytes of storage are to be used for the program in the virtual partition. If you don't know how much storage to request, you can code SIZE=AUTO and DOS/VS will calculate the proper amount, *except* when the COBOL program contains a SORT statement. Then you can code SIZE=(AUTO,nK), where n is a minimum of 16 (the system will add the K amount on to the value it calculates). The remainder of the virtual partition is used by the VSAM modules required by your program. You must code the SIZE operand for every program that uses VSAM files.

To illustrate, consider figure 6-3. Here, the SELECT statements and JCL are given for a file-creation program similar to the one in figure 2-10. As you can see, the INVMSTR SELECT statement assigns the inventory master file to logical unit SYS020. In the JCL, the DLBL statement for the inventory file supplies the filename

The SELECT statements

```
SELECT INVCRDS ASSIGN TO SYS005-UR-2540R-S.
SELECT INVMSTR ASSIGN TO SYS020-INVMSTR
               ORGANIZATION IS INDEXED
               ACCESS IS RANDOM
               RECORD KEY IS IM-ITEM-NUMBER
               FILE STATUS IS INVMSTR-ERROR-CODE.
```

The JCL

```
// JOB     INVCR
// DLBL    INVMSTR,'INVENTORY MASTER FILE',,VSAM
// EXEC    INVCR,SIZE=AUTO
           data
/*
/&
```

Figure 6-3 SELECT statements and JCL required for a DOS file-loading program

(INVMSTR), the file identification ('INVENTORY MASTER FILE'), and the VSAM code to indicate the file is a VSAM file.

I hope you can appreciate the simplicity of this JCL. If the inventory file were an ISAM file, the JCL would be considerably more complicated. Up to four EXTENT statements are required to create an ISAM file if a master index and general overflow areas are used. And these EXTENT statements must supply relative track addresses and lengths for each of the ISAM areas used. Under VSAM, all of this information is specified via IDCAMS, so it isn't necessary to code it in the JCL.

For DOS/VS and VSE versions earlier than release 2, an EXTENT statement is required for VSAM files. At the minimum, the EXTENT statement must specify the file's logical unit (SYSnnn), and it may also specify the volume name. Normally, the volume name should be left off the EXTENT statement. Then, if the file is moved to a different volume, the JCL doesn't have to be changed.

The ISAM interface program

Like OS, DOS provides an ISAM interface program that allows your ISAM programs to process VSAM files without modification. To use the DOS ISAM interface, simply code the usual VSAM JCL (as in figures 6-2 and 6-3). When DOS opens the file expecting it to be an ISAM file and finds a VSAM file instead, it automatically invokes the ISAM interface to process the file. Figure 6-4 shows an example of a job that uses an ISAM file and the same job after the file has been converted to VSAM. The only change is in the JCL; the program itself remains unchanged.

Again, I would like to discourage the use of the ISAM interface program. Although it is intended to be a first step towards conversion to VSAM, it is often seen as the final step. If you're going to use the ISAM interface, remember that it is only a temporary solution. As soon as possible, you should modify your programs to process VSAM files directly, without the ISAM interface.

DOS ACCESS-METHODS-SERVICES

Under DOS, IDCAMS is used to perform all VSAM utility functions just as it is for OS. In order to execute IDCAMS under DOS, you must code an EXEC statement like this:

```
// EXEC IDCAMS,SIZE=26K
```

The SIZE parameter must be coded or IDCAMS won't execute. 26K is the size recommendation given in the DOS IDCAMS manual. Before the EXEC statement, you must place any necessary JCL statements to properly define the files that will be processed by IDCAMS. You'll see examples of these JCL statements in just a moment. Following the EXEC statement, you place the IDCAMS control statements. For the most part, the control statements are the

A job to process an ISAM file

```
// JOB      UPMAST
// TLBL     FORTIPT,'INPUT TRANS'
// DLBL     FORTAB,'FORMTBL',,ISE
// EXTENT SYS020,TSTPAK,4,1,2600,10
// EXTENT SYS020,TSTPAK,1,2,2620,400
// EXTENT SYS020,TSTPAK,1,2,3020,180
// EXEC     UPMAST
/&
```

A job executing the same program to process a VSAM file

```
// JOB      UPMAST
// TLBL     FORTIPT,'INPUT TRANS'
// DLBL     FORTAB,'FORMTAB',,VSAM
// EXEC     UPMAST,SIZE=AUTO
/&
```

Figure 6-4 Using the DOS ISAM interface

same for DOS as they are for OS. However, there are a few minor variations.

The following examples show how to set up DOS jobs to define a data space, define a cluster, load a cluster from an ISAM file, print a cluster, and perform routine catalog maintenance. These examples are simply DOS versions of the OS IDCAMS jobs already presented.

Defining a data space

Figure 6-5 shows a DOS job for defining a VSAM data space. In this job, the DEFINE statement uses only two parameters. TRACKS specifies the number of tracks to be allocated to the space, and VOLUMES specifies the name of the volume that will contain the space. Incidentally, on a DOS system, both VOLUME and VOLUMES are acceptable keywords in a DEFINE statement.

If you want to specify the starting track for a data space, you code the ORIGIN parameter, like this:

```
DEFINE SPACE -
 (ORIGIN(19) -
  TRACKS(209) -
  VOLUMES(DOST21) )
```

In this case, the data space is 209 tracks long starting at track 19. If the ORIGIN parameter is omitted, IDCAMS selects the first track that fulfills the space requirements specified. For this reason, it is usually best to omit the ORIGIN parameter and let IDCAMS do the work for you.

On DOS/VS systems and DOS/VSE systems earlier than release 2, you must specify a DLBL and EXTENT statement to define the volume. The EXTENT statement must specify the space allocation information for the data space. And the FILE parameter is required in the DEFINE statement to identify the DLBL statement that defines the volume, like this:

```
DEFINE SPACE -
 (TRACKS(209) -
  VOLUMES(DOST21) -
  FILE(VOL1) )
```

In this case, VOL1 must be the file name in a DLBL statement that defines the space on DOST21.

Defining a cluster

Figure 6-6 shows how to define a VSAM key-sequenced cluster on a DOS system. Here, an indexed file named INVMSTR is defined on a volume named DOST21. The primary allocation is 100 records, as is

```
// JOB     LOWE
// EXEC    IDCAMS,SIZE=26K
   DEFINE SPACE -
            (TRACKS(209) -
             VOLUME (DOST21) )
/*
/&
```

Figure 6-5 Defining a data space

```
// JOB     LOWE
// EXEC    IDCAMS,SIZE=26K
   DEFINE CLUSTER -
            (NAME(INVMSTR) -
             VOLUMES(DOST21) -
             RECORDS(100 100) -
             RECORDSIZE(32 32) -
             INDEXED -
             KEYS(5 1) )
/*
/&
```

Figure 6-6 Defining a key-sequenced cluster

the secondary allocation, so the maximum size of the file is 1,600 records. The records are a fixed length of 32 bytes, with the keys in the first five bytes of each record. Because the file will be placed in an existing data space, no DLBL or EXTENT statements are required. If there is no space on the volume, a DLBL and EXTENT statement can be included (with space allocation specified) and a space will be generated automatically when the cluster is defined. In this case, a FILE parameter must be coded on the DEFINE statement to identify the DLBL statement defining the volume. (Unlike OS, the UNIQUE parameter is not required to cause a data space to be generated.) On a DOS version earlier than VSE release 2, the DLBL and EXTENT statements and the FILE parameter must be coded even if the data space already exists.

Copying VSAM files

Figure 6-7 shows a job that copies a VSAM file named INVMSTR to another VSAM file named INVMSTR2. Here, the REPRO command specifies the input and output files in the INFILE and OUTFILE parameters. Both files must be defined with a DLBL statement. (On

```
// JOB     LOWE
// DLBL    INVMSTR,'INVMSTR',,VSAM
// DLBL    INVMSTR2,'INVMSTR2',,VSAM
// EXEC    IDCAMS,SIZE=26K
   REPRO INFILE(INVMSTR) -
         OUTFILE(INVMSTR2)
/*
/&
```

Figure 6-7 Copying a VSAM file

versions earlier than VSE release 2, an EXTENT statement is required as well.)

Loading a VSAM file from an ISAM file

Figure 6-8 shows how to load a VSAM file from a non-VSAM file, in this case an ISAM file. The first DLBL statement and its three EXTENT statements define the ISAM file: it is named ISMSTR and resides on disk volume 231401. The next DLBL statement defines the VSAM file (INVMSTR). The REPRO statement specifies the ISAM file as input and the VSAM file as output. There is one important difference in the operation of the REPRO command for OS and DOS: under OS, the REPRO command automatically removes dummy ISAM records as the file is copied; under DOS, dummy records are copied over along with the live records. So in order to remove dummy records from an ISAM file on a DOS system, you must first reorganize it.

Printing a VSAM file

Figure 6-9 illustrates an IDCAMS job that prints the contents of a key-sequenced VSAM file in CHARACTER format. Here, the DLBL statement defines the VSAM input file. In the PRINT statement, the INFILE parameter specifies the name supplied on the DLBL statement. The CHARACTER parameter specifies the output format; DUMP and HEX may be coded instead to achieve a different output format.

Maintaining catalogs

Figure 6-10 presents a DOS job that uses the DELETE, ALTER, and DEFINE NONVSAM statements to perform routine VSAM catalog maintenance. The DELETE statement simply causes the entry for

```
// JOB     LOWE
// DLBL    INDD,'ISMSTR',,ISE
// EXTENT  SYS013,231401,4,1,20,20
// EXTENT  SYS013,231401,1,2,40,20
// EXTENT  SYS013,231401,2,3,60,20
// DLBL    INVMSTR,'INVMSTR',,VSAM
// EXEC    IDCAMS,SIZE=26K
   REPRO INFILE(INDD) -
         OUTFILE(INVMSTR)
/*
/&
```

Figure 6-8 Loading a VSAM file from a non-VSAM file

```
// JOB     LOWE
// DLBL    INVMSTR,'INVMSTR',,VSAM
// EXEC    IDCAMS,SIZE=26K
   PRINT INFILE(INVMSTR) -
         CHARACTER
/*
/&
```

Figure 6-9 Printing a VSAM file in CHARACTER format

```
// JOB     LOWE
// EXEC    IDCAMS,SIZE=26K
   DELETE (INVMSTR)
   ALTER  (ARMAST) -
            NEWNAME(ARMSTR)
   DEFINE NONVSAM -
            (NAME(BJTRAN) -
             DEVICETYPES(3330) -
             VOLUMES(DOST36)
/*
/&
```

Figure 6-10 Maintaining a catalog

INVMSTR to be removed from the catalog. The ALTER statement changes the name of ARMAST to ARMSTR. The DEFINE NON-VSAM statement causes a non-VSAM file named BJTRAN on a 3330 volume named DOSTR36 to be cataloged in the VSAM catalog.

DISCUSSION

In most cases, VSAM processing is the same whether you are working on an OS or a DOS system. From a COBOL standpoint, the only difference is the assignment name in the SELECT statement and the JCL. And most of the IDCAMS control statements are the same, although the JCL is considerably different. So if you grasp the concepts presented in the rest of this book, you should now be able to apply these concepts on DOS systems.

Objectives

1. Given a programming problem involving VSAM files, code an acceptable solution in DOS COBOL.
2. Given reference material, code the DOS JCL required to execute a program that processes a VSAM file.
3. Given reference material, code a DOS IDCAMS job to define a VSAM space or cluster, copy or print a VSAM file, or perform routine VSAM catalog maintenance.

Problems

The following problems are taken from earlier chapters in this book. They have been modified for DOS.

1. (Chapter 2, Topic 1) Suppose you have written a COBOL program that processes a VSAM file named GMPAYRL. Code the JCL statements necessary to define this file. The file's identification should be 'PAYROLL MASTER FILE'.
2. (Chapter 2, Topic 2) Assume an ISAM inventory-master file was converted to VSAM three months before the inventory-file maintenance program was modified to process it as a VSAM file. In the meantime, the ISAM version of the maintenance program was used to process the VSAM file using the ISAM interface. Now, because of the way the ISAM program handled deletions, the VSAM file contains several hundred inactive records, indicated by the delete code (HIGH-VALUE) in the first byte of each deleted record. Write a COBOL program to reorganize the file by deleting all the records marked as inactive. The format of the inventory record is this:

Field name	Delete code	Item no.	Item description	On hand	Unused
Characteristics	X	X(5)	X(20)	S9(5)	X(3)
Usage				COMP-3	
Position	1	2-6	7-26	27-29	30-32

Each time a record is deleted, display a message showing the record's item number. The VSAM file should be assigned to logical unit SYS020 and its file name should be VSAMSTR.

3. (Chapter 2, Topic 3) Figure 2-10 is an indexed file-creation program coded for an OS system. Make the necessary changes to this program so that it properly handles error conditions. When an unrecoverable I/O error occurs, the program should be terminated and a storage dump should be printed. So the program in figure 2-10 will run under DOS, change the ASSIGN clause of the SELECT statement to this:

```
ASSIGN TO SYS020-INVMSTR
```

4. (Chapter 4) Code the necessary changes to the file-creation program in figure 2-10 so that the file being loaded is an entry-sequenced file rather than a key-sequenced file. Assume that the file may or may not already have records in it; if there are records in the file, the new records should be added to the end. Also, change the error processing so that if any type of read error occurs, the program displays a message indicating the item number and the FILE STATUS field and terminates the program via the CANCEL subprogram.

Solutions

1. Here is an acceptable solution:

```
// DLBL GMPAYRL,'PAYROLL MASTER FILE',,VSAM
```

2. Figure 2-19 is an acceptable solution for OS COBOL. For DOS COBOL, the assignment name in the ASSIGN clause of the SELECT statement should be:

```
SYS020-VSAMSTR
```

3. Figure 2-23 is an acceptable solution for OS COBOL. For the program to run properly on a DOS system, two changes must be made. First, the SELECT statement must be changed as indicated in the problem definition. Second, the subprogram name in the CALL statement must be changed from ABEND200 to DUMP.
4. Figure 4-5 is an acceptable solution for OS COBOL. For the program to run properly on a DOS system, two changes must be made. First, the SELECT statement for the VSAM file must be changed so that the assignment name follows the DOS format. Second, the subprogram name in the CALL statement must be changed to CANCEL.

Appendix

ISAM/VSAM Conversion Guide

This appendix is designed to help you convert your existing ISAM programs so they process VSAM files. It presents all of the ISAM processing elements available on the version 4 compiler along with the corresponding VSAM elements available on the VS compiler. You will also find a notation for each modification that must be made to your ISAM program.

ISAM format	VSAM format	Notes
FILE-CONTROL.	FILE-CONTROL.	
SELECT file-name	SELECT file-name	
ASSIGN TO DA-I-file name	ASSIGN TO [comments-]filename	Remove DA-I in ASSIGN clause.
	ORGANIZATION IS INDEXED	Add ORGANIZATION clause.
ACCESS MODE IS {SEQUENTIAL / RANDOM}	ACCESS MODE IS {SEQUENTIAL / RANDOM}	
NOMINAL KEY IS data-name		Remove NOMINAL KEY clause.
RECORD KEY IS data-name	RECORD KEY IS data-name	
TRACK AREA IS {data-name / integer} CHARACTERS		Remove TRACK AREA clause.
	FILE STATUS is data-name	Add FILE STATUS clause.
I-O-CONTROL.	I-O-CONTROL.	
RERUN ON system-name EVERY integer RECORDS OF file-name.	RERUN ON system-name EVERY integer RECORDS OF file-name.	
SAME RECORD AREAS FOR file-name...	SAME RECORD AREAS FOR file-name...	
APPLY WRITE-ONLY ON file-name.		Remove WRITE-ONLY statement.
APPLY CORE-INDEX ON file-name.		Remove CORE-INDEX statement.
APPLY REORG-CRITERIA TO data-name ON file-name.		Remove REORG-CRITERIA statement.
DATA DIVISION.	DATA DIVISION.	
FILE SECTION.	FILE SECTION.	
FD file-name	FD file-name	
LABEL RECORDS ARE {STANDARD / OMITTED}	LABEL RECORDS ARE {STANDARD / OMITTED}	
RECORDING MODE IS {F / V}		Remove the RECORDING MODE clause.
RECORD CONTAINS integer CHARACTERS	RECORD CONTAINS integer CHARACTERS	
BLOCK CONTAINS integer RECORDS		Remove the BLOCK CONTAINS clause.
DATA RECORDS ARE data-name...	DATA RECORDS ARE data-name...	
WORKING-STORAGE SECTION.	WORKING-STORAGE SECTION.	
(Definition of NOMINAL KEY field)		NOMINAL KEY field isn't required.
	(Definition of FILE STATUS field)	Add definition of FILE STATUS field.

ISAM format	VSAM format	Notes
PROCEDURE DIVISION. START file-name INVALID KEY imperative-statement	PROCEDURE DIVISION. START file-name KEY IS { EQUAL TO / = / GREATER THAN / > / NOT LESS THAN / NOT < } data-name [INVALID KEY imperative-statement]	KEY clause has been expanded.
Invalid key clause: INVALID KEY imperative-statement	Invalid key clause: [INVALID KEY imperative-statement]	Invalid key clause isn't required if an IF statement is used to test for FILE STATUS conditions.
Nominal key processing		All processing on NOMINAL KEY field should be modified to process RECORD KEY field. Use cross-reference listing to locate NOMINAL KEY field references.

Index

Comment Form

Your opinions count

If you have comments, criticisms, or suggestions, I'm eager to get them. Your opinions today will affect our products of tomorrow. If you have questions, you can expect an answer within one week from the time we receive them. And if you discover any errors in this product, typographical or otherwise, please point them out so we can make corrections when the product is reprinted.

Thanks for your help.

Mike Murach
Fresno, California

fold

fold

Book title: VSAM for the COBOL Programmer

Dear Mike: ______________________________

fold

fold

Name and Title ____________________

Company (if any) ____________________

Address ____________________

City, State, & Zip ____________________

Fold where indicated and seal.
No postage necessary if mailed in the United States.

fold

fold

NO POSTAGE
NECESSARY
IF MAILED
IN THE
UNITED STATES

BUSINESS REPLY MAIL

First Class Permit No. 3063 Fresno, CA

POSTAGE WILL BE PAID BY ADDRESSEE

Mike Murach & Associates, Inc.

4222 West Alamos, Suite 101

Fresno, California 93711

fold

fold

Order Form

Our Unlimited Guarantee

To our customers who order directly from us: You must be satisfied. Our books must work for you, or you can send them back for a full refund...no matter how many you buy, no matter how long you've had them.

Name & Title ______________________

Company (if any) ______________________

Address ______________________

City, State, Zip ______________________

Phone number (including area code) ______________________

Qty.	Product code and title		Price
CICS and VSAM			
____	CIC1	CICS for the COBOL Programmer: Part 1	$25.00
____	VSAM	VSAM for the COBOL Programmer	15.00
COBOL Language Elements			
____	CAG	COBOL Advisor's Guide	$100.00
____	SAC1	Structured ANS COBOL: Part 1	20.00
____	SAC2	Structured ANS COBOL: Part 2	20.00
____	RW	Report Writer	13.50
COBOL Program Development			
____	DDCP	How to Design and Develop COBOL Programs	$20.00
____	CPHB	The COBOL Programmer's Handbook	20.00
Other (please specify)			
____	____________		
____	____________		

Qty.	Product code and title		Price
System Development			
____	DDBS	How to Design and Develop Business Systems	$20.00
____	SDCS	System Development Case Studies	6.00
____	SDIG	System Development Instructor's Guide	35.00
OS Subjects			
____	TSO	MVS TSO	$22.50
____	OJCL	OS JCL	22.50
____	OSUT	OS Utilities	15.00
____	OSDB	OS Debugging for the COBOL Programmer	20.00
Assembler Language			
____	ASMD	DOS Assembler Language	$22.50
____	ASMO	OS Assembler Language	22.50
Other (please specify)			
____	____________		
____	____________		

☐ Bill me the appropriate price plus shipping and handling (and sales tax in California) for each book ordered.

☐ I want to **save** shipping and handling charges. Here's my check or money order for $________. California residents, please add 6% sales tax to your total. (Offer valid in the U.S. only.)

☐ Bill the appropriate book prices plus shipping and handling (and sales tax in California) to my
_____ Visa _____ MasterCard:

Card number ______________________

Valid thru (month/year) ______________________

Cardowner's signature ______________________
(not valid without signature)

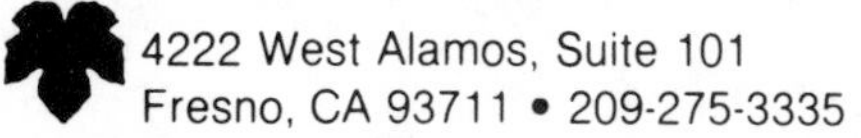

4222 West Alamos, Suite 101
Fresno, CA 93711 • 209-275-3335

To order more quickly,

Call **toll-free** 1-800-221-5528
In California, call 1-800-221-5527

fold

fold

NO POSTAGE
NECESSARY
IF MAILED
IN THE
UNITED STATES

BUSINESS REPLY MAIL

First Class Permit No. 3063 Fresno, CA

POSTAGE WILL BE PAID BY ADDRESSEE

Mike Murach & Associates, Inc.

4222 West Alamos, Suite 101

Fresno, California 93711

fold

fold